one pot

& slow cooking

essential recipes

Publisher's Note:
Raw or semi-cooked eggs should not be consumed by babies, toddlers, pregnant or breast-feeding women, the elderly or those suffering from recurring illness.

Recipe Note:
All eggs and vegetables are medium sized, unless otherwise stated.

Publisher and Creative Director: Nick Wells
Project Editor: Cat Emslie
Copy Editor: Kathy Steer
Photographers: Colin Bowling, Paul Forrester and Stephen Brayne
Home Economists & Stylists: Ann Nicol, Jaqueline Bellefontaine,
Mandy Phipps, Vicki Smallwood and Penny Stephens
Art Director: Mike Spender
Layout Design: Dave Jones
Digital Design and Production: Chris Herbert and Claire Walker
Proofreader: Alison Bolus

12 11

7 9 10 8 6

This edition first published 2008 by
FLAME TREE PUBLISHING
Crabtree Hall, Crabtree Lane
Fulham, London SW6 6TY
United Kingdom

www.flametreepublishing.com

Flame Tree is part of the Foundry Creative Media Co. Ltd

© 2008 this edition The Foundry Creative Media Co. Ltd

ISBN 978-1-84786-996-8

A CIP record for this book is available from the British Library upon request.

Printed in China

one pot

& slow cooking

essential recipes

General Editor: Gina Steer

FLAME TREE
PUBLISHING

Contents

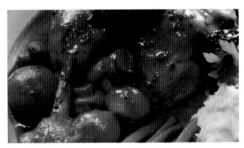

Fish & Seafood

Vegetables

Hygiene in the Kitchen

It is important to remember that many foods can carry some form of bacteria. In most cases, the worst it will lead to is a bout of food poisoning or gastroenteritis, although for certain people this can be serious. The risk can be reduced or eliminated, however, by good hygiene and proper cooking.

Do not buy food that is past its sell-by date and do not consume food that is past its use-by date. When buying food, use your eyes and nose: if the food looks tired, limp or a bad colour or it has a rank, acrid or simply bad smell, do not buy or eat it under any circumstances.

Dish cloths and tea towels must be washed and changed regularly. Ideally, use disposable cloths and replace on a daily basis. More durable cloths should be left to soak in bleach, then washed in the washing machine at a high temperature. Keep hands, utensils and food preparation surfaces clean and do not allow pets to climb on to work surfaces. Avoid handling food if suffering from an upset stomach, as bacteria can be passed on through food preparation.

Buying

Avoid bulk buying where possible, especially fresh produce. Fresh foods lose their nutritional value rapidly, so buying a little at a time minimises loss of nutrients. Check that any packaging is intact and not damaged or pierced at all. Store fresh foods in the refrigerator as soon as possible.

When buying frozen foods, ensure that they are not heavily iced on the outside and that the contents feel completely frozen. Ensure that they have been stored in the cabinet at the correct storage level and the temperature is below -18°C/-0.4°F. Pack in cool bags to transport home and place in the freezer as soon as possible after purchase.

Preparation

Take special care when preparing raw meat and fish. Separate chopping boards should be used for each, and the knife, board and your hands should be thoroughly washed before handling or preparing any other food. Good-quality plastic boards are available in various designs and colours. This makes differentiating easier and the plastic has the added hygienic advantage of being washable at high temperatures in the dishwasher. If using the board for fish, first wash in cold water, then in hot to prevent odour.

When cooking, be particularly careful to keep cooked and raw food separate to avoid any contamination. It is worth washing all fruits and vegetables regardless of whether they are going to be eaten raw or lightly cooked. This rule should apply even to prewashed herbs and salads.

Do not reheat food more than once. If using a microwave, always check that the food is piping hot all the way through – in theory, the food should reach 70°C/158°F and needs to be cooked at that temperature for at least three minutes to ensure that all bacteria are killed.

All poultry must be thoroughly thawed before using. Remove the food to be thawed from the freezer and place in a shallow dish to contain the juices. Leave the food in the refrigerator until it is completely thawed. A 1.4 kg/3 lb whole chicken will take about 26–30 hours to thaw. To speed up the process, immerse the chicken in cold water, making sure that the water is changed regularly. When the joints can move freely and no ice crystals remain in the cavity, the bird is completely thawed. Once thawed, remove the wrapper and pat dry. Place the chicken in a shallow dish, cover lightly

and store as close to the base of the refrigerator as possible. The chicken should be cooked as soon as possible.

Some foods can be cooked from frozen including many prepacked foods such as soups, sauces, casseroles and breads. Where applicable, follow the manufacturers' instructions. Vegetables and fruits can also be cooked from frozen, but meats and fish should be thawed first. The only time food can be refrozen is when the food has been thoroughly thawed then cooked. Once the food has cooled, it can be frozen again, but it should only be stored for one month.

All poultry and game (except for duck) must be cooked thoroughly. When cooked, the juices will run clear on the thickest part of the bird – the best area to try is usually the thigh. Other meats, like beef, lamb and pork, should be cooked right the way through. Fish should turn opaque, be firm in texture and break easily into large flakes.

Make sure leftovers are reheated until piping hot and that any sauce or soup reaches boiling point first.

Storing, Refrigerating and Freezing

Meat, poultry, fish, seafood and dairy products should all be refrigerated. The temperature of the refrigerator should be between 1–5°C/34–41°F, while the freezer temperature should not rise above -18°C/-0.4°F. To ensure the optimum temperature, avoid leaving the door open for long periods. Try not to overstock, as this reduces the airflow inside and therefore the effectiveness in cooling the food within.

When refrigerating cooked food, allow it to cool down quickly and completely before refrigerating. Hot food will raise the temperature of the refrigerator and possibly affect or spoil other food stored in it.

Food should always be covered. Raw and cooked food should be stored in separate parts of the refrigerator. Cooked food should be kept on the top shelves, while raw meat, poultry and fish should be placed on the bottom to avoid drips and cross-contamination. It is recommended that eggs be refrigerated in order to maintain their freshness and shelf life.

Regularly clean, defrost and clear out the refrigerator and freezer – it is worth checking the packaging to see exactly how long each product is safe to freeze. Take care that frozen foods are not stored in the freezer for too long. Blanched vegetables can be stored for one month; beef, lamb, poultry and pork for six months and unblanched vegetables and fruits in syrup for a year. Oily fish and sausages should be stored for no more than three months. Dairy products can last four to six months, while cakes and pastries can be kept in the freezer for three to six months.

High-risk Foods

Certain foods may carry risks to people who are considered vulnerable, such as the elderly, the ill, pregnant women, babies, young infants and those suffering from a recurring illness.

There is a slight chance that some eggs carry the bacteria salmonella. Cook the eggs until both the yolk and the white are firm to eliminate this risk. Pay particular attention to dishes and products incorporating lightly cooked or raw eggs, such as hollandaise sauce, mayonnaise, mousses, soufflés, meringues, custard-based dishes, ice creams and sorbets. Certain meats and poultry also carry the potential risk of salmonella and so should be cooked thoroughly until the juices run clear and there is no pinkness left. Unpasteurised products such as milk, cheese (especially soft cheese), pâté, meat (raw and cooked) all have the potential risk of listeria and should be avoided.

When buying seafood, buy from a reputable source which has a high turnover to ensure freshness. Fish should have bright clear eyes, shiny skin and bright pink or red gills. The fish should feel stiff to the touch, with a slight smell of sea air. The flesh of fish steaks and fillets should be translucent with no signs of discolouration. Molluscs such as scallops, and mussels are sold fresh and are still alive. Avoid any that are open or do not close when tapped lightly, also discard any that do not open after cooking. In the same way, univalves such as cockles or winkles should withdraw back into their shells when lightly prodded. When choosing cephalopods such as squid, check that they have a firm flesh and pleasant sea smell.

As with all fish, whether it is shellfish or seafish, care is required when freezing it. It is imperative to check whether the fish has been frozen before. If it has been frozen, then it should not be frozen again under any circumstances.

Nutrition: The Role of Essential Nutrients

A healthy and well-balanced diet is the body's primary energy source. In children, it constitutes the building blocks for future health as well as providing lots of energy. In adults, it encourages self-healing and regeneration within the body. A well-balanced diet will provide the body with all the essential nutrients it needs. This can be achieved by eating a variety of foods, demonstrated in the pyramid below.

FATS

PROTEINS

milk, yogurt   meat, fish, poultry,
and cheese   eggs, nuts and pulses

FRUITS AND
VEGETABLES

STARCHY CARBOHYDRATES

cereals, potatoes, bread, rice and pasta

FATS

Fats fall into two categories: saturated and unsaturated. Fats are an essential part of the diet as they are a source of energy and provide essential fatty acids and fat-soluble vitamins, but it is very important that a healthy balance is achieved. The right balance should boost the body's immunity to infection and keep muscles, nerves and arteries in good condition. Saturated fats are of animal origin and can be found in dairy produce, meat, eggs, margarines and hard white cooking fat (lard) as well as in manufactured products such as pies, biscuits and cakes. A high intake of saturated fat over many years has been proven to increase heart disease and high blood cholesterol levels and often leads to weight gain. Lowering the amount of saturated fat that we consume is very important, but this does not mean that it is good to consume lots of other types of fat.

There are two kinds of unsaturated fats: polyunsaturated and monounsaturated. Polyunsaturated fats include safflower, soya bean, corn and sesame oils. The Omega-3 oils in polyunsaturated fats have been found to be beneficial to coronary health and can encourage brain growth and development. They are derived from oily fish such as salmon, mackerel, herring, pilchards and sardines. It is recommended that we should eat these types of fish at least once a week. Alternative liver oil supplements are also available. The most popular oils that are high in monounsaturates are olive oil, sunflower oil and peanut oil. Monounsaturated fats are also known to help reduce the levels of cholesterol.

PROTEINS

Composed of amino acids – proteins' building blocks – proteins perform a wide variety of essential functions for the body, including supplying energy and building and repairing tissues. Good sources of proteins are eggs, milk, yogurt, cheese, meat, fish, poultry, eggs, nuts and pulses. (See the second level of the pyramid.) Some of these foods, however, contain saturated fats. To strike a nutritional balance, eat generous amounts of vegetable protein foods such as soya, beans, lentils, peas and nuts.

MINERALS

CALCIUM Important for healthy bones and teeth, nerve transmission, muscle contraction, blood clotting and hormone function. Also promotes a healthy heart and skin, relieves aching muscles and bones, maintains the correct acid–alkaline balance and reduces menstrual cramps. Good sources are dairy products, small bones of small fish, nuts, pulses, fortified white flours, breads and green leafy vegetables.

CHROMIUM Balances blood sugar levels, helps to reduce cravings, improves lifespan, helps protect DNA and is essential for heart function. Good sources are brewer's yeast, wholemeal bread, rye bread, oysters, potatoes, green peppers, butter and parsnips.

IODINE Important for the manufacture of thyroid hormones and for normal development. Good sources are seafood, seaweed, milk and dairy.

IRON As a component of haemoglobin, iron carries oxygen around the body. It is vital for normal growth and development. Good sources are liver, corned beef, red meat, fortified breakfast cereals, pulses, green leafy vegetables, egg yolk, cocoa and cocoa products.

MAGNESIUM Important for efficient functioning of metabolic enzymes and development of the skeleton. Magnesium promotes healthy muscles by helping them to relax and is therefore good for PMS. It is also important for heart muscles and the nervous system. Good sources are nuts, green vegetables, meat, cereals, milk and yogurt.

PHOSPHORUS Forms and maintains bones and teeth, builds muscle tissue, helps maintain pH of the body and aids metabolism and energy production. Phosphorus is present in almost all foods.

POTASSIUM Enables processing of nutrients; promotes healthy nerves and muscles; maintains fluid balance; helps secretion of insulin for blood sugar control; relaxes muscles; maintains heart functioning and stimulates gut movement. Good sources are fruit, vegetables, milk and bread.

SELENIUM Antioxidant properties help to protect against free radicals and carcinogens. Selenium reduces inflammation, stimulates the immune system, promotes a healthy heart and helps vitamin E's action. Necessary for the male reproductive system and for metabolism. Good sources are tuna, liver, kidney, meat, eggs, cereals, nuts and dairy products.

SODIUM Important in helping to control body fluid, preventing dehydration. Sodium is involved in muscle and nerve function and helps move nutrients into cells. All foods are good sources. Processed, pickled and salted foods are richest in sodium but should be eaten in moderation.

ZINC Important for metabolism and healing; aids ability to cope with stress; promotes a healthy nervous system and brain, especially in the growing foetus; aids bone and teeth formation and is essential for energy. Good sources are liver, meat, pulses, whole-grain cereals, nuts and oysters.

VITAMINS

BIOTIN Important for metabolism of fatty acids. Good sources of biotin are liver, kidney, eggs and nuts.

FOLIC ACID Critical during pregnancy for the development of the brain and nerves. It is always essential for brain and nerve function and is needed for utilising protein and red blood cell formation. Good sources are whole-grain cereals, fortified cereals, green leafy vegetables, oranges and liver.

VITAMIN A Important for cell growth and development and for the formation of visual pigments in the eye. Vitamin A comes in two forms: retinol and beta-carotene. Retinol is found in liver, meat and whole milk. Beta-carotene is a powerful antioxidant and is found in red and yellow fruits and vegetables such as carrots, mangoes and apricots.

VITAMIN B1 Important in releasing energy from carbohydrate-containing foods. Good sources are yeast and yeast products, bread, fortified breakfast cereals and potatoes.

VITAMIN B2 Important for metabolism of proteins, fats and carbohydrates to produce energy. Good sources are meat, yeast extracts, fortified breakfast cereals and milk and its products.

VITAMIN B3 Required for the metabolism of food into energy. Good sources are milk, fortified cereals, pulses, meat, poultry and eggs.

VITAMIN B5 Important for the metabolism of food and energy production. All foods are good sources but especially fortified breakfast cereals, whole-grain bread and dairy products.

VITAMIN B6 Important for metabolism of protein and fat. Vitamin B6 may also be involved in the regulation of sex hormones. Good sources are liver, fish, pork, soya beans and peanuts.

VITAMIN B12 Important for the production of red blood cells and DNA. It is vital for growth and the nervous system. Good sources are meat, fish, eggs, poultry and milk.

VITAMIN C Important for healing wounds and the formation of collagen, which keeps skin and bones strong. It is an important antioxidant. Good sources are fruits, especially soft summer fruits, and vegetables.

VITAMIN D Important for absorption and handling of calcium to help build bone strength. Good sources are oily fish, eggs, whole milk and milk products, margarine and, of course, sufficient exposure to sunlight, as vitamin D is made in the skin.

VITAMIN E Important as an antioxidant vitamin helping to protect cell membranes from damage. Good sources are vegetable oils, margarines, seeds, nuts and green vegetables.

VITAMIN K Important for controlling blood clotting. Good sources are cauliflower, Brussels sprouts, lettuce, cabbage, beans, broccoli, peas, asparagus, potatoes, corn oil, tomatoes and milk.

CARBOHYDRATES

Carbohydrates are an energy source and come in two forms: starch and sugar. Starch carbohydrates are also known as complex carbohydrates and they include all cereals, potatoes, breads, rice and pasta. Eating whole-grain varieties of these foods also provides fibre. Diets high in fibre are believed to be beneficial in helping to prevent bowel cancer and keep cholesterol down. Sugar carbohydrates – also known as fast-release because they provide a quick fix of energy – include sugar and sugar-sweetened products. Other sugars are lactose (from milk) and fructose (from fruit).

Meat

Looking to fill your home with the savoury smells of an old-fashioned, hearty meal? Beef Bourguignon and Chilli Con Carne are must tries. Looking for a change of pace? Pork with Tofu & Coconut could be the answer. If you have cast-iron cookware that can be used on the hob as well as in the oven, then you will truly be 'one pot' cooking; if not, use a pan on the hob and then transfer to an oven-proof casserole to get the 'slow-cooked' style.

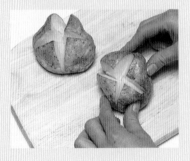

Vietnamese Beef & Rice Noodle Soup

1 Place all the ingredients for the beef stock into a large stock pot or saucepan and cover with cold water. Bring to the boil and skim off any scum that rises to the surface. Reduce the heat and simmer gently, partially covered, for 2–3 hours, skimming occasionally.

2 Strain into a large bowl and leave to cool, then skim off the fat. Cover and chill in the refrigerator and, when cold, remove any fat from the surface. Pour 1.7 litres/3 pints of the stock into a large wok or saucepan and reserve.

3 Place the noodles in a mixing bowl, cover with warm water and leave for 3 minutes or until just softened. Drain, then cut into 10 cm/4 inch lengths.

4 Arrange the spring onions and chilli on a serving platter or large plate. Strip the leaves from the coriander and mint and arrange them in piles on the plate.

5 Bring the stock in the wok or saucepan to the boil over a high heat. Add the noodles and simmer for about 2 minutes or until tender. Add the beef strips and simmer for about 1 minute. Season to taste with salt and pepper.

6 Ladle the soup with the noodles and beef strips into individual soup bowls and serve immediately with the plate of condiments handed around separately.

Ingredients SERVES 4–6

For the beef stock:
900 g/2 lb meaty beef bones
1 large onion, peeled and quartered
2 carrots, peeled and cut into chunks
2 celery stalks, trimmed and sliced
1 leek, washed and sliced into chunks
2 garlic cloves, left whole and
    lightly crushed
3 whole star anise
1 tsp black peppercorns

For the condiment:
4–6 spring onions, trimmed
    and diagonally sliced
1 red chilli, deseeded and
    diagonally sliced
1 small bunch fresh coriander
1 small bunch fresh mint

For the soup:
175 g/6 oz dried rice stick noodles
350 g/12 oz fillet steak,
    very thinly sliced
salt and freshly ground black pepper

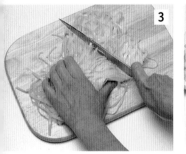

Chinese Leaf & Mushroom Soup

1 Trim the stem ends of the Chinese leaves and cut in half lengthways. Remove the triangular core with a knife, then cut into 2.5 cm/1 inch slices and reserve.

2 Place the dried shiitake mushrooms in a bowl and pour over enough almost-boiling water to cover. Leave to stand for 20 minutes to soften, then gently lift them out and squeeze out the liquid. Discard the stems and thinly slice the caps and reserve. Strain the liquid through a muslin-lined sieve or a coffee filter paper and reserve.

3 Heat a wok over a medium-high heat, add the oil and when hot add the bacon. Stir-fry for 3–4 minutes or until crisp and golden, stirring frequently. Add the ginger and chestnut mushrooms and stir-fry for a further 2–3 minutes.

4 Add the chicken stock and bring to the boil, skimming any fat and scum that rise to the surface. Add the spring onions, sherry or rice wine, Chinese leaves, sliced shiitake mushrooms and season to taste with salt and pepper. Pour in the reserved soaking liquid and reduce the heat to the lowest possible setting.

5 Simmer gently, covered, until all the vegetables are very tender; this will take about 10 minutes. Add a little water if the liquid has reduced too much. Spoon into soup bowls and drizzle with a little sesame oil. Serve immediately.

Ingredients   SERVES 4–6

450 g/1 lb Chinese leaves
25 g/1 oz dried shiitake mushrooms
1 tbsp vegetable oil
75 g/3 oz smoked streaky
    bacon, diced
2.5 cm/1 inch piece fresh root
    ginger, peeled and finely chopped
175 g/6 oz chestnut mushrooms,
    wiped and thinly sliced
1.1 litres/2 pints chicken stock
4–6 spring onions, trimmed and
    cut into short lengths
2 tbsp dry sherry or Chinese
    rice wine
salt and freshly ground black pepper
sesame oil for drizzling

Tasty tip

If Chinese leaves are not available, use Savoy cabbage.

Classic Minestrone

1 Heat the butter and olive oil together in a large saucepan. Add the bacon to the saucepan. Cook for 3–4 minutes, then remove with a slotted spoon and reserve.

2 Add the onion, garlic, celery and carrots to the saucepan, one at a time, stirring well after each addition. Cover and cook gently for 8–10 minutes, until the vegetables are softened.

3 Add the chopped tomatoes, with their juice and the stock, bring to the boil, then cover the saucepan with a lid, reduce the heat and simmer gently for about 20 minutes.

4 Stir in the cabbage, beans, peas and spaghetti pieces. Cover and simmer for a further 20 minutes or until all the ingredients are tender. Season to taste with salt and pepper.

5 Return the cooked bacon to the saucepan and bring the soup to the boil. Serve the soup immediately with Parmesan cheese shavings sprinkled on the top and plenty of crusty bread to accompany it.

Ingredients SERVES 6–8

25 g/1 oz butter

3 tbsp olive oil

3 rashers streaky bacon, diced

1 large onion, peeled and finely chopped

1 garlic clove, peeled and finely chopped

1 celery stick, trimmed and finely chopped

2 carrots, peeled and finely chopped

400 g/14 oz can chopped tomatoes

1.1 litres/2 pints good-quality chicken stock

175 g/6 oz green cabbage, outer leaves and central core discarded and finely shredded

50 g/2 oz French beans, trimmed and halved

3 tbsp frozen petits pois

50 g/2 oz spaghetti, broken into pieces

salt and freshly ground black pepper

Parmesan cheese shavings, to garnish

crusty bread, to serve

Beef Bourguignon

1 Preheat the oven 160°C/325°F/Gas Mark 3. Cut the steak and pork into small pieces and reserve. Heat 1 tablespoon of the oil in an ovenproof casserole (or frying pan, if preferred), add the meat and cook in batches for 5–8 minutes, or until sealed. Remove with a slotted spoon and reserve.

2 Add the remaining oil to the casserole/pan, then add the shallots, carrots and garlic and cook for 10 minutes. Return the meat to the casserole/pan and sprinkle in the flour. Cook for 2 minutes, stirring occasionally, before pouring in the brandy. Heat for 1 minute, then take off the heat and ignite.

3 When the flames have subsided, pour in the wine and stock. Return to the heat and bring to the boil, stirring constantly.

4 If a frying pan has been used, transfer everything to a casserole, add the bay leaf and season to taste with salt and pepper. Cover with a lid and cook in the oven for 1 hour.

5 Cut the potatoes in half. Remove the casserole from the oven and add the potatoes. Cook for a further 1 hour, or until the meat and potatoes are tender. Serve sprinkled with chopped parsley.

Ingredients SERVES 4

675 g/1½ lb braising steak, trimmed
225 g/8 oz piece of pork belly
   or lardons
2 tbsp olive oil
12 shallots, peeled
2 garlic cloves, peeled and sliced
225 g/8 oz carrots, peeled and sliced
2 tbsp plain flour
3 tbsp brandy (optional)
150 ml/¼ pint red wine, such
   as a Burgundy
450 ml/¾ pint beef stock
1 bay leaf
salt and freshly ground black pepper
450 g/1 lb new potatoes, scrubbed
1 tbsp freshly chopped parsley,
   to garnish

Tasty tip

If time allows, increase the wine to 300 ml/½ pint and marinate the beef in the refrigerator overnight.

Steak & Kidney Stew

1   Heat the oil in a large, heavy-based saucepan, add the onion, garlic and celery and sauté for 5 minutes, or until browned. Remove from the pan with a slotted spoon and reserve.

2   Add the steak and kidneys to the pan and cook for 3–5 minutes, or until sealed, then return the onion mixture to the pan. Sprinkle in the flour and cook, stirring, for 2 minutes. Take off the heat, stir in the tomato purée, then the stock, and season to taste with salt and pepper. Add the bay leaf.

3   Return to the heat and bring to the boil, stirring occasionally. Add the carrots, then reduce the heat to a simmer and cover with a lid. Cook for 1¼ hours, stirring occasionally. Reduce the heat if the liquid is evaporating quickly. Add the potatoes and cook for a further 30 minutes.

4   Place the flour, suet and herbs in a bowl and add a little seasoning. Add the water and mix to a stiff mixture. Using a little extra flour, shape into 8 small balls. Place the dumplings on top of the stew, cover with the lid and continue to cook for 15 minutes, or until the meat is tender and the dumplings are well risen and fluffy. Stir in the spinach and leave to stand for 2 minutes, or until the spinach is wilted.

Ingredients   SERVES 4

1 tbsp olive oil
1 onion, peeled and chopped
2–3 garlic cloves, peeled and crushed
2 celery sticks, trimmed and sliced
550 g/1¼ lb braising steak, trimmed
  and diced
100 g/4 oz lambs' kidneys, cored
  and chopped
2 tbsp plain flour
1 tbsp tomato purée
900 ml/1½ pints beef stock
salt and freshly ground black pepper
1 fresh bay leaf
300 g/10 oz carrots, peeled and sliced
350 g/12 oz baby new
  potatoes, scrubbed
350 g/12 oz fresh spinach
  leaves, chopped

For the dumplings:

100 g/4 oz self-raising flour
50 g/2 oz shredded suet
1 tbsp freshly chopped mixed herbs
2–3 tbsp water

Italian Beef Pot Roast

1 Preheat oven to 150°C/300°F/Gas Mark 2, 10 minutes before cooking. Place the beef in a bowl. Add the onions, garlic, celery and carrots. Make a cross in the top of each tomato and place in a bowl. Cover with boiling water and allow to stand for 2 minutes, then drain. Leave until cool enough to handle, then peel away the skins. Cut into quarters and discard the seeds. Chop, then add to the bowl with the red wine. Cover tightly and marinate in the refrigerator overnight.

2 Lift the marinated beef from the bowl and pat dry with absorbent kitchen paper. Heat the olive oil in a large casserole and cook the beef until it is browned all over, then remove. Drain the vegetables from the marinade, reserving the marinade. Add the vegetables to the casserole and fry gently for 5 minutes, stirring occasionally, until all the vegetables are browned.

3 Return the beef to the casserole with the marinade, beef stock, tomato purée and mixed herbs and season with salt and pepper. Bring to the boil, then cover and cook in the preheated oven for 3 hours.

4 Using a slotted spoon, transfer the beef and any large vegetables to a plate and leave in a warm place. Blend the butter and flour to form a paste. Bring the casserole juices to the boil and then gradually stir in small spoonfuls of the paste. Cook until thickened. Serve with the meat and reserved vegetables.

Ingredients   SERVES 6

1.8 kg/4 lb brisket of beef
225 g/8 oz small onions, peeled
3 garlic cloves, peeled and chopped
2 celery sticks, trimmed and chopped
2 carrots, peeled and sliced
450 g/1 lb ripe tomatoes
300 ml/¹/₂ pint Italian red wine
2 tbsp olive oil
300 ml/¹/₂ pint beef stock
1 tbsp tomato purée
2 tsp freeze-dried mixed herbs
salt and freshly ground black pepper
25 g/1 oz butter
25 g/1 oz plain flour
freshly cooked vegetables, to serve

Helpful hint

Most supermarkets do not sell brisket, but good butchers will be able to order it. Brisket is an excellent cut for all kinds of pot roasts, but make sure it is professionally trimmed as it can contain a lot of gristle and fat

Chilli Con Carne with Crispy-skinned Potatoes

1 Preheat the oven to 180°C/350°F/Gas Mark 4. Heat the oil in a large ovenproof casserole and add the onion. Cook gently for 10 minutes until soft and lightly browned. Add the garlic and chilli and cook briefly. Increase the heat, add the chuck steak or lean mince and cook for a further 10 minutes, stirring occasionally, until browned.

2 Add the chilli powder and stir well. Cook for about 2 minutes, then add the chopped tomatoes and tomato purée. Bring slowly to the boil. Cover and cook in the preheated oven for 1 hour. Remove the chilli from the oven and stir in the kidney beans. Return to the oven for a further 15 minutes.

3 Meanwhile, brush a little vegetable oil all over the potatoes and rub on some coarse salt. Put the potatoes in the oven alongside the chilli.

4 Remove the chilli from the oven and stir in the kidney beans. Return to the oven for a further 15 minutes.

5 Remove the chilli and potatoes from the oven. Cut a cross in each potato, then squeeze to open slightly and season to taste with salt and pepper. Serve with the chilli, guacamole and soured cream.

Ingredients   SERVES 4

2 tbsp vegetable oil, plus extra
　　for brushing
1 large onion, peeled and
　　finely chopped
1 garlic clove, peeled and
　　finely chopped
1 red chilli, deseeded and
　　finely chopped
450 g/1 lb chuck steak, finely
　　chopped, or lean beef mince
1 tbsp chilli powder
400 g/14 oz can chopped tomatoes
2 tbsp tomato purée
400 g/14 oz can red kidney beans,
　　drained and rinsed
4 large baking potatoes
coarse salt and freshly ground
　　black pepper to serve:
ready-made guacamole
soured cream

Beef Fajitas with Avocado Salsa

1   Heat a wok or large saucepan, add the oil, then stir-fry the beef for 3–4 minutes. Add the garlic and spices and continue to cook for a further 2 minutes. Stir the tomatoes into the wok or pan, bring to the boil, cover and simmer gently for 5 minutes.

2   Meanwhile, blend the kidney beans in a food processor until slightly broken up, then add to the wok or pan. Continue to cook for a further 5 minutes, adding 2–3 tablespoons of water. The mixture should be thick and fairly dry. Stir in the chopped coriander.

3   Make the avocado salsa by mixing the chopped avocado, shallot, tomato, chilli and lemon juice together. Spoon into a serving dish and reserve.

4   When ready to serve, warm the tortillas as directed on the packet and spread with a little soured cream. Place a spoonful of the beef mixture on top, followed by a spoonful of the avocado sauce, then roll up. Repeat until all the mixture is used up. Serve immediately with a green salad.

Ingredients   SERVES 3–6

2 tbsp sunflower oil
450 g/1 lb beef fillet or rump steak, trimmed and cut into thin strips
2 garlic cloves, peeled and crushed
1 tsp ground cumin
$^1/_4$ tsp cayenne pepper
1 tbsp paprika
230 g/8 oz can chopped tomatoes
215 g/7$^1/_2$ oz can red kidney beans, drained and rinsed
1 tbsp freshly chopped coriander
6 large flour tortillas
3–4 tbsp soured cream
green salad, to serve

For the salsa:

1 avocado, peeled, pitted and chopped
1 shallot, peeled and chopped
1 large tomato, skinned, deseeded and chopped
1 red chilli, deseeded and diced
1 tbsp lemon juice

Lamb and Date Tagine

1 Place the saffron in a small bowl, cover with warm water and leave to infuse for 10 minutes. Heat the oil in a large, heavy-based pan, add the onion, garlic and lamb and sauté for 8–10 minutes, or until sealed. Add the cinnamon stick and ground cumin and cook, stirring constantly, for a further 2 minutes.

2 Add the carrots and sweet potato, then add the saffron with the soaking liquid and the stock. Bring to the boil, season to taste with salt and pepper, then reduce the heat to a simmer. Cover with a lid and simmer for 45 minutes, stirring occasionally.

3 Add the dates and continue to simmer for a further 15 minutes. Remove the cinnamon stick, adjust the seasoning and serve with freshly prepared couscous.

Ingredients SERVES 4

few saffron strands
1 tbsp olive oil
1 onion, peeled and cut into wedges
2–3 garlic cloves, peeled and sliced
550 g/1¼ lb lean lamb such as
  neck fillet, diced
1 cinnamon stick, bruised
1 tsp ground cumin
225 g/8 oz carrots, peeled and sliced
350 g/12 oz sweet potato,
  peeled and diced
900 ml/1½ pints lamb or
  vegetable stock
salt and freshly ground black pepper
100 g/4 oz dates (fresh or dried),
  pitted and halved
freshly prepared couscous, to serve

Tasty tip

Replace the dates with chopped ready-to-eat dried apricots.

Lancashire Hotpot

1. Preheat the oven to 170°C/325°F/Gas Mark 3. Trim any excess fat from the lamb cutlets. Heat the oil in an ovenproof casserole and brown the cutlets in batches for 3–4 minutes. Remove with a slotted spoon and reserve. Add the onions to the casserole and cook for 6–8 minutes until softened and just beginning to colour, then remove and reserve.

2. Stir in the flour and cook for a few seconds, then gradually pour in the stock, stirring well, and bring to the boil. Pour into a jug and reserve. Rinse the casserole to clean, and wipe dry.

3. Spread the base of the casserole with half the potato slices. Top with half the onions and season well with salt and pepper. Arrange the browned meat in a layer. Season again and add the remaining onions, bay leaf and thyme. Pour in all the reserved gravy and top with the remaining potatoes so that they overlap in a single layer. Brush the potatoes with the melted butter and season again.

4. Cover the casserole and cook in the preheated oven for 2 hours, uncovering for the last 30 minutes to allow the potatoes to brown. Garnish with chopped herbs and serve immediately with green beans.

Ingredients   SERVES 4

1 kg/2¼ lb middle end neck of lamb, divided into cutlets
2 tbsp vegetable oil
2 large onions, peeled and sliced
2 tsp plain flour
150 ml/¼ pint vegetable or lamb stock
700 g/1½ lb waxy potatoes, peeled and thickly sliced
salt and freshly ground black pepper
1 bay leaf
2 sprigs fresh thyme
1 tbsp melted butter
2 tbsp freshly chopped herbs, to garnish
freshly cooked green beans, to serve

Food fact

The name of this classic dish derives from the past tradition of wrapping it in blankets after cooking to keep it warm until lunchtime. There are many versions, all claiming to be authentic. Some include lambs kidneys to enrich the gravy, but whatever the ingredients, it is important to season well and to cook it slowly, so that the lamb is meltingly tender.

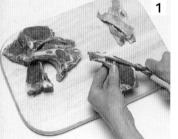

Lamb Pilaf

1. Preheat the oven to 170°C/325°F/Gas Mark 3. Heat the oil in an ovenproof casserole with a tight-fitting lid and add the almonds. Fry for about 1 minute until just starting to brown, stirring often. Add the onion, carrot and celery and cook gently for a further 8–10 minutes, until soft and lightly browned.

2. Increase the heat and add the lamb. Cook for a further 5 minutes until the lamb has changed colour. Add the ground cinnamon and chilli flakes and stir briefly before adding the tomatoes and orange rind.

3. Stir and add the rice, then the stock. Bring slowly to the boil and cover tightly. Transfer to the preheated oven and cook for 30–35 minutes until the rice is tender and the stock is absorbed.

4. Remove from the oven and leave to stand for 5 minutes before stirring in the chives and coriander. Season to taste with salt and pepper. Garnish with the lemon slices and sprigs of fresh coriander and serve immediately.

Ingredients   SERVES 4

2 tbsp vegetable oil
25 g/1 oz flaked or almonds
1 onion, peeled and finely chopped
1 carrot, peeled and finely chopped
1 celery stick, trimmed and
  finely chopped
350 g/12 oz lean lamb, cut into chunks
$1/4$ tsp ground cinnamon
$1/4$-$1/2$ tsp crushed chilli flakes
2 large tomatoes, skinned,
  deseeded and chopped
grated rind of 1 orange
350 g/12 oz easy-cook brown
  basmati rice
600 ml/1 pint vegetable or lamb stock
2 tbsp freshly snipped chives
3 tbsp freshly chopped coriander
salt and freshly ground black pepper

To garnish:
lemon slices
sprigs of fresh coriander

Cawl

1   Put the lamb in a large saucepan, cover with cold water and bring to the boil. Add a generous pinch of salt. Simmer gently for 1¹/₂ hours, then leave until cool. Cover and leave in the refrigerator overnight.

2   The next day, skim the fat off the surface of the lamb liquid and discard. Return the saucepan to the heat and bring back to the boil. Simmer for 5 minutes. Add the onions, potatoes, parsnips, swede and carrots and return to the boil. Reduce the heat, cover and cook for 20 minutes, stirring occasionally.

3   Add the leeks and season to taste with salt and pepper. Cook for a further 10 minutes or until all the vegetables are tender.

4   Using a slotted spoon, remove the meat from the saucepan and leave to cool for a while, then take the meat off the bones. Discard the bones and any gristle, then return the meat to the pan. Adjust the seasoning to taste, stir in the parsley, then serve immediately with plenty of warm crusty bread.

Ingredients   SERVES 4–6

700 g/1¹/₂ lb scrag end of lamb
  or best end of neck chops
pinch of salt
2 large onions, peeled and
  thinly sliced
3 large potatoes, peeled and cut
  into chunks
2 parsnips, peeled and cut
  into chunks
1 swede, peeled and cut into chunks
3 large carrots, peeled and cut
  into chunks
2 leeks, trimmed and sliced
freshly ground black pepper
4 tbsp freshly chopped parsley
warm crusty bread, to serve

Cassoulet

1. Preheat the oven to 180°C/350°F/Gas Mark 4. Heat the oil in a large saucepan or ovenproof casserole, add the onion, celery, carrot and garlic and sauté for 5 minutes. Cut the pork, if using, into small pieces and cut the sausages into chunks.

2. Add the meat to the vegetables and cook, stirring, until lightly browned.

3. Add the thyme sprigs and season to taste with salt and pepper. If a saucepan was used, transfer everything to an ovenproof casserole.

4. Spoon the beans on top, then pour in the stock. Mix the breadcrumbs with 1 tablespoon of the chopped thyme in a small bowl and sprinkle on top of the beans. Cover with a lid and cook in the oven for 40 minutes. Remove the lid and cook for a further 15 minutes, or until the breadcrumbs are crisp. Sprinkle with the remaining chopped thyme and serve.

Ingredients   SERVES 4

1 tbsp olive oil
1 onion, peeled and chopped
2 celery sticks, trimmed and chopped
175 g/6 oz carrots, peeled and sliced
2–3 garlic cloves, peeled and crushed
350 g/12 oz pork belly (optional)
8 spicy thick sausages,
    such as Toulouse
few sprigs of fresh thyme
salt and freshly ground black pepper
2 x 400 g/14 oz cans cannellini
    beans, drained and rinsed
600 ml/1 pint vegetable stock
75 g/3 oz fresh breadcrumbs
2 tbsp freshly chopped thyme

Tasty tip
Replace the pork belly with lardons, if you prefer.

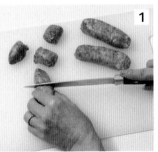

Sausage & Apple Pot

1 Preheat the oven to 180°C/350°F/Gas Mark 4. Heat the oil in an ovenproof casserole (or frying pan, if preferred), add the onion, garlic and celery and sauté for 5 minutes. Push the vegetables to one side then add the sausages and cook, turning the sausages over, until browned.

2 If a frying pan has been used, transfer everything to a casserole. Arrange the onions over and around the sausages together with the carrots, apple and courgettes. Season to taste with salt and pepper and pour over the stock. Sprinkle with the mixed herbs, cover with a lid and cook in the oven for 30 minutes.

3 Meanwhile, soak the grated potatoes in a bowl of cold water for 10 minutes. Drain thoroughly, then place the potatoes on a clean tea towel and squeeze to remove any excess moisture.

4 Remove the casserole from the oven and place the grated potatoes on top. Sprinkle with the grated cheese, then return to the oven and cook for 30 minutes, or until the vegetables are tender and the topping is crisp.

Ingredients
SERVES 4

1 tbsp olive oil
1 onion, peeled and sliced
2–3 garlic cloves, peeled and sliced
2 celery sticks, trimmed and sliced
8 apple- and pork-flavoured
  thick sausages
300 g/10 oz carrots, peeled
  and sliced
1 large cooking apple, peeled
  and sliced
300 g/10 oz courgettes, trimmed
  and sliced
salt and freshly ground black pepper
600 ml/1 pint vegetable stock
2 tsp dried mixed herbs
450 g/1 lb potatoes, peeled
  and grated
50 g/2 oz Gruyère cheese, grated

Tasty tip
Other flavoured sausages can be used according to personal preference, such as herb, chilli or Cumberland. Vegetarian sausages can also be used.

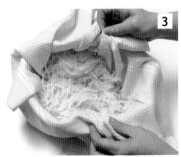

New Orleans Jambalaya

1 Mix all the seasoning ingredients together in a small bowl and reserve.

2 Heat 2 tablespoons of the oil in a large flameproof casserole over a medium heat. Add the ham and sausage and cook, stirring often, for 7–8 minutes until golden. Remove from the pan and reserve.

3 Add the remaining oil and the onions, celery and peppers to the casserole and cook for about 4 minutes, or until the vegetables have softened, stirring occasionally. Stir in the garlic, then, using a slotted spoon, transfer all the vegetables to a plate and reserve with the sausage.

4 Add the chicken pieces to the casserole and cook for about 5-7 minutes, or until beginning to colour, turning once. Stir in the seasoning mix and turn the pieces to coat well. Return the sausage and vegetables to the casserole and stir well. Add the chopped tomatoes, with their juice, and the stock and bring to the boil.

5 Stir in the rice and reduce the heat to low. Cover and simmer for 12 minutes. Uncover, stir in the spring onions and prawns and cook, covered, for a further 4 minutes. Add the crab and gently stir in. Cook for 2–3 minutes, or until the chicken and rice are tender. Remove from the heat, remove the bay leaves, cover and leave to stand for 5 minutes before serving.

Ingredients   SERVES 6–8

For the seasoning mix:

2 dried bay leaves
1 tsp salt
2 tsp cayenne pepper, or to taste
2 tsp dried oregano
1 tsp each ground white and black
    pepper, or to taste

For the Jambalaya:

3 tbsp vegetable oil
100 g/4 oz ham, fat discarded, and diced
225 g/8 oz smoked pork sausage,
    cut into chunks
2 large onions, peeled and chopped
4 celery sticks, trimmed and chopped
2 green peppers, deseeded and chopped
2 garlic cloves, peeled and finely chopped
350 g/12 oz boneless chicken thighs,
    skinned and diced
400 g/14 oz can chopped tomatoes
600 ml/1 pint fish stock
400 g/14 oz long-grain white rice
4 spring onions, trimmed and chopped
275 g/10 oz raw prawns, peeled
250 g/9 oz white crab meat

Oven-roasted Vegetables with Sausages

1 Preheat the oven to 200°C/400°F/Gas Mark 6, 15 minutes before cooking. Line a large roasting tin with foil and pour in the olive oil then heat in the preheated oven for 3 minutes, or until very hot. Add the aubergines, courgettes and garlic cloves, then stir until coated in the hot oil and cook in the oven for 10 minutes.

2 Remove the roasting tin from the oven and stir. Lightly prick the sausages, add to the roasting tin and return to the oven. Continue to roast for a further 20 minutes, turning once during cooking, until the vegetables are tender and the sausages are golden brown.

3 Meanwhile, roughly chop the plum tomatoes and drain, then rinse, the cannellini beans. Remove the sausages from the oven and stir in the tomatoes and cannellini beans. Season to taste with salt and pepper, then return to the oven for 5 minutes, or until heated thoroughly.

4 Scatter over the basil leaves and sprinkle with plenty of Parmesan cheese and extra freshly ground black pepper. Serve immediately.

Ingredients   SERVES 4

3 tbsp olive oil
2 aubergines, trimmed and cut into
   bite-sized chunks
3 courgettes, trimmed and cut into
   bite-sized chunks
6 garlic cloves, unpeeled
8 Tuscany-style sausages
4 plum tomatoes
2 x 300 g/10½ oz cans
   cannellini beans
salt and freshly ground black pepper
1 small bunch fresh basil, torn into
   coarse pieces
4 tbsp freshly grated
   Parmesan cheese

Helpful hint

By leaving the garlic cloves unpeeled a more delicate flavour is achieved. If a more robust flavour is required, peel the garlic before cooking.

Pork Goulash

1 Preheat the oven to 170°C/325°F/Gas Mark 3. Cut the pork into large cubes, about 4 cm/1½ inches square. Heat the oil in a large ovenproof casserole and brown the pork in batches over a high heat, transferring the cubes to a plate as they brown.

2 Over a medium heat, add the onions and pepper and cook for about 5 minutes, stirring regularly, until they begin to brown. Add the garlic and return the meat to the casserole along with any juices on the plate. Sprinkle in the flour and paprika and stir well to soak up the oil and juices.

3 Add the tomatoes and season to taste with salt and pepper. Bring slowly to the boil, cover with a tight-fitting lid and cook in the preheated oven for 1½-2 hours or until tender. Heat the rice according to the packet instructions.

4 When the meat is tender, stir in the soured cream lightly to create a marbled effect, or serve separately. Garnish with parsley and serve immediately with the rice.

Ingredients   SERVES 6

700 g/1½ lb boneless pork rib chops
1 tbsp olive oil
2 onions, peeled and
    roughly chopped
1 red pepper, deseeded and
    sliced thinly
1 garlic clove, peeled and crushed
1 tbsp plain flour
1 rounded tbsp paprika
400 g/14 oz can chopped tomatoes
salt and freshly ground black pepper
2 x 250 g/9 oz pkts microwaveable
    long-grain rice
150 ml/¼ pt soured cream
sprigs of fresh parsley

Food fact

Paprika is the ground red powder from the dried pepper *Capsicum annum* and is a vital ingredient of goulash, giving it a distinctive colour and taste.

Spanish-style Pork Stew

1 Preheat the oven to 170°C/325°F/Gas Mark 3. Heat the oil in a large ovenproof casserole and add the pork in batches. Fry over a high heat until browned. Transfer to a plate until all the pork is browned.

2 Lower the heat and add the onion to the casserole. Cook for a further 5 minutes until soft and starting to brown. Add the garlic and stir briefly before returning the pork to the casserole. Add the flour and stir.

3 Add the tomatoes. Gradually stir in the red wine and stock then add the basil. Bring to simmering point and cover. Transfer the casserole to the lower part of the preheated oven and cook for 1½ hours. Stir in the green pepper and olives and cook for 30 minutes or until tender. Adjust the seasoning. Heat the rice according to the packet instructions and serve the pork garnished with fresh basil.

Ingredients   SERVES 4

2 tbsp olive oil
675 g/1½ lb boneless pork
   shoulder, diced
1 large onion, peeled and sliced
2 garlic cloves, peeled and
   finely chopped
1 tbsp plain flour
450 g/1 lb plum tomatoes, peeled
   and chopped
175 ml/6 fl oz red wine
150 ml/¼ pt vegetable stock
1 tbsp freshly chopped basil
1 green pepper, deseeded and sliced
50 g/2 oz pimiento-stuffed olives,
   cut in half crossways
salt and freshly ground black pepper
fresh basil leaves, to garnish
2 x 250g/9 oz pkts microwaveable
   basmati rice, to serve

Pork Chop Hotpot

1 Preheat the oven to 190°C/375°F/Gas Mark 5, 10 minutes before cooking. Trim the pork chops, removing any excess fat and rind, wipe with a clean, damp cloth, then dust with a little flour and reserve. Cut the shallots in half, if large. Chop the garlic and slice the sun-dried tomatoes.

2 Heat the olive oil in a large casserole dish and cook the pork chops for about 5-8 minutes or until sealed, turning the chops over once. Remove from the casserole and reserve, Add the shallots to the oil remaining in the casserole and cook, stirring occasionally, for 5 minutes.

3 Return the pork chops to the casserole and scatter with the garlic and sun-dried tomatoes, then pour over the can of tomatoes with their juice.

4 Blend the red wine, stock and tomato purée together and add the chopped oregano. Season to taste with salt and pepper, then pour over the pork chops and bring to a gentle boil. Cover with a close-fitting lid and cook in the preheated oven for 20 minutes. Add the potatoes (if using at this point) to the casserole and continue to cook for 40 minutes or until the pork chops and potatoes are tender. Adjust the seasoning to taste, then scatter with a few oregano leaves and serve immediately, with separate new potatoes (if preferred) and French beans, if liked.

Ingredients   SERVES 4

4 pork chops (bone-in)
flour, for dusting
225 g/8 oz shallots, peeled
2 garlic cloves, peeled
50 g/2 oz sun-dried tomatoes in oil
2 tbsp olive oil
400 g/14 oz can plum tomatoes
150 ml/¼ pint red wine
150 ml/¼ pint chicken stock
3 tbsp tomato purée
2 tbsp freshly chopped oregano
salt and freshly ground black pepper
450 g/1 lb new potatoes, scrubbed
    and halved, if large (optional,
    see below)
fresh oregano leaves, to garnish
freshly cooked new potatoes, to
    serve (if preferred separately)
French beans, to serve (optional)

Oven-baked Pork Balls with Peppers

1   Preheat the oven to 200°C/400°F/Gas Mark 6, 15 minutes before cooking. If making your own garlic bread, crush the garlic, then blend with the softened butter, the parsley and enough lemon juice to give a soft consistency. Shape into a roll, wrap in baking parchment paper and chill in the refrigerator for at least 30 minutes.

2   Mix together the pork, basil, 1 chopped garlic clove, sun-dried tomatoes and seasoning until well combined. With damp hands, divide the mixture into 16, roll into balls and reserve.

3   Spoon the olive oil in a large roasting tin (lined with foil if liked) and place in the preheated oven for about 3 minutes, until very hot. Remove from the heat and stir in the pork balls, the remaining chopped garlic and peppers. Bake for about 15 minutes. Remove from the oven and stir in the cherry tomatoes and season to taste with plenty of salt and pepper. Bake for about a further 20 minutes.

4   Just before the pork balls are ready, either heat the bought garlic bread (if using) according to packet instructions, or, if making your own, slice the bread, toast lightly and spread with the prepared garlic butter. Remove the pork balls from the oven, stir in the vinegar and serve immediately with the garlic bread.

Ingredients   SERVES 4

For the garlic bread (optional):
2–4 garlic cloves, peeled
50 g/2 oz butter, softened
1 tbsp freshly chopped parsley
2–3 tsp lemon juice
1 focaccia loaf

For the pork balls:
450 g/1 lb fresh pork mince
4 tbsp freshly chopped basil
2 garlic cloves, peeled and chopped
3 sun-dried tomatoes, chopped
salt and freshly ground black pepper
3 tbsp olive oil
1 medium red pepper, deseeded and
   cut into chunks
1 medium green pepper, deseeded
   and cut into chunks
1 medium yellow pepper, deseeded
   and cut into chunks
225 g/8 oz cherry tomatoes
2 tbsp balsamic vinegar

bought garlic bread, to serve (if not
   making own)

Italian Risotto

1 Heat the olive oil in a large frying pan and cook the salami or speck for 3–5 minutes, or until golden. Using a slotted spoon, transfer to a plate and keep warm. Add the asparagus and stir-fry for 2–3 minutes, until just wilted. Transfer to the plate with the salami. Add the onion and garlic and cook for 5 minutes, or until softened.

2 Add the rice to the pan and cook for about 2 minutes, stirring frequently. Add the wine and bring to the boil, then simmer, stirring until the wine has been absorbed. Add half the stock and return to the boil. Simmer, stirring until the liquid has been absorbed.

3 Add half of the remaining stock and the broad beans to the rice mixture. Bring to the boil, then simmer for a further 5–10 minutes, or until all of the liquid has been absorbed.

4 Add the remaining stock, bring to the boil, then simmer until all the liquid is absorbed and the rice is tender. Stir in the remaining ingredients until the cheese has just melted. Serve immediately.

Ingredients   SERVES 4

1 tbsp olive oil
100 g/4 oz Italian salami
    or speck, chopped
100 g/4 oz asparagus, trimmed
    and cut into short lengths
1 onion, peeled and chopped
2 garlic cloves, peeled and chopped
350 g/12 oz risotto rice
300 ml/$^{1}/_{2}$ pt dry white wine
1 litre/$1^{3}/_{4}$ pints chicken stock, warmed
125 g/4 oz frozen broad beans,
    defrosted
125 g/4 oz Dolcelatte cheese, diced
3 tbsp freshly chopped mixed herbs,
    such as parsley and basil
salt and freshly ground black pepper

Food fact

Cheese is a common constituent in the making of risotto and in fact helps to provide some of its creamy texture. Usually Parmesan cheese is added at the end of cooking, but here a good-quality Dolcelatte is used instead.

Risi e Bisi

1 Shell the peas, if using fresh ones. Melt the butter and olive oil together in a large, heavy-based saucepan. Add the chopped pancetta or bacon, the chopped onion and garlic and gently fry for about 10 minutes, or until the onion is softened and is just beginning to colour.

2 Add the caster sugar, lemon juice and bay leaf, then pour in the vegetable stock. Add the fresh peas, if using. Bring the mixture to a fast boil.

3 Add the rice, stir and simmer, uncovered, for about 20 minutes, or until the rice is tender. Occasionally, stir the mixture gently while it cooks. If using frozen petits pois, stir them into the rice about 2 minutes before the end of the cooking time.

4 When the rice is cooked, remove the bay leaf and discard. Stir in $2\frac{1}{2}$ tablespoons of the chopped parsley and the grated Parmesan cheese. Season to taste with salt and pepper.

5 Transfer the rice to a large serving dish. Garnish with the remaining chopped parsley, and the strips of orange rind. Serve immediately while piping hot.

Ingredients   SERVES 4

700 g/1½ lb young peas in pods or
   175 g/6 oz frozen petits pois, thawed
25 g/1 oz unsalted butter
1 tsp olive oil
3 rashers pancetta or unsmoked
   back bacon, chopped
1 small onion, peeled and finely chopped
1 garlic clove, peeled and finely chopped
pinch of caster sugar
1 tsp lemon juice
1 bay leaf
1.3 litres/2¼ pints vegetable stock
200 g/7 oz risotto rice
3 tbsp freshly chopped parsley
50 g/2 oz Parmesan cheese, finely grated
salt and freshly ground black pepper

To garnish:

sprig of fresh parsley
julienne strips of orange rind

Leek & Ham Risotto

1   Heat the oil and half the butter together in a large saucepan. Add the onion and leeks and cook over a medium heat for 6–8 minutes, stirring occasionally, until soft and beginning to colour. Stir in the thyme and cook briefly.

2   Add the rice and stir well. Continue stirring over a medium heat for about 1 minute until the rice is glossy. Add a ladleful or two of the stock and stir well until the stock is absorbed. Continue adding stock, a ladleful at a time, and stirring well between additions, until about two-thirds of the stock has been added.

3   Meanwhile, either chop or finely shred the ham, then add to the rice together with the peas. Continue adding ladlefuls of stock, as described in step 2, until the rice is tender and the ham is heated through thoroughly.

4   Add the remaining butter, sprinkle over the Parmesan cheese and season to taste with salt and pepper. When the butter has melted and the cheese has softened, stir well to incorporate. Taste and adjust the seasoning, then serve immediately.

Ingredients   SERVES 4

1 tbsp olive oil
25 g/1 oz butter
1 onion, peeled and finely chopped
4 leeks, trimmed and thinly sliced,
   plus extra to garnish
1¹/₂ tbsp freshly chopped thyme
350 g/12 oz risotto rice
1.4 litres/2¹/₂ pints vegetable
   or chicken stock, heated
225 g/8 oz cooked ham
175 g/6 oz peas, thawed if frozen
50 g/2 oz Parmesan cheese, grated
salt and freshly ground black pepper

Helpful hint

Risotto should take about 20-25 minutes to cook, so taste it after this time – the rice should be creamy with just a slight bite to it. If it is not quite ready, continue adding the stock, a little at a time, and cook for a few more minutes. Stop as soon as it tastes ready, as you do not have to add all of the liquid.

Sausage & Bacon Risotto

1 Heat a wok or large frying pan, add the oil and melt the butter. Cook the cocktail sausages for 8-10 minutes or until cooked, turning continuously. Remove with a slotted spoon, cut in half and keep warm.

2 Add the chopped shallot and bacon to the wok or frying pan and cook for 2–3 minutes until cooked but not browned. Add the chorizo or spicy sausage and green pepper and stir-fry for a further 3 minutes.

3 Add the cold rice and the sweetcorn to the wok or frying pan and stir-fry for 2 minutes, then return the cooked sausages and cook over the heat until everything is piping hot. Garnish with the freshly chopped parsley and serve immediately.

Ingredients   SERVES 4

1 tbsp vegetable oil
25 g/1 oz butter
175 g/6 oz cocktail sausages
1 shallot, peeled and finely chopped
75 g/3 oz bacon lardons or thick
   slices of streaky bacon, chopped
150 g/5 oz chorizo or similar spicy
   sausage, cut into chunks
1 green pepper, deseeded and
   cut into strips
300 g/10 oz precooked long-
   grain rice
197 g/7 oz can sweetcorn, drained
2 tbsp freshly chopped parsley

Helpful hint

It is now possible to buy packets of bacon or pancetta lardons, but if these are unavailable, try to get bacon in a piece from a butcher or deli. Cut the bacon into 1 cm/$\frac{1}{2}$ inch slices then cut the slices crossways into 1 cm/$\frac{1}{2}$ inch pieces.

Honey Pork with Rice Noodles & Cashews

1 Place the noodles in a large bowl and cover with boiling water for 4 minutes or according to the packet instructions, then drain and reserve.

2 Trim and slice the pork fillet into thin strips. Heat the wok (or separate frying pan if you'd rather), pour in the oil and butter, and stir-fry the pork for 4–5 minutes, until cooked. Remove with a slotted spoon and keep warm.

3 Add the onion to the wok and stir-fry gently for 2 minutes. Stir in the garlic and mushrooms and cook for a further 2 minutes, or until the juices start to run from the mushrooms.

4 Blend the soy sauce with the honey, then return the pork to the wok with this mixture. Add the cashew nuts and cook for 1–2 minutes, then add the rice noodles a little at a time. Stir-fry until everything is piping hot. Sprinkle with chopped chilli and spring onions. Serve immediately with freshly stir-fried vegetables.

Ingredients   SERVES 4

100 g/4 oz rice noodles
450 g/1 lb pork fillet
2 tbsp groundnut oil
15 g/½ oz softened butter
1 onion, peeled and finely sliced
   into rings
2 garlic cloves, peeled and crushed
100 g/4 oz baby button mushrooms,
   halved
3 tbsp light soy sauce
3 tbsp clear honey
50 g/2 oz unsalted cashew nuts
1 red chilli, deseeded and
   finely chopped
4 spring onions, trimmed and
   finely chopped
freshly stir-fried vegetables, to serve
curls of spring onion, to garnish

Pork with Tofu & Coconut

1　Place the cashew nuts, coriander, cumin, chilli powder, ginger and oyster sauce in a food processor and blend until well ground. Heat a wok or large frying pan, add 2 tablespoons of the oil and, when hot, add the cashew mixture and stir-fry for 1 minute. Stir in the coconut milk and bring to the boil, then simmer for 1 minute. Pour into a small jug and reserve. Wipe the wok clean.

2　Meanwhile, place the rice noodles in a bowl and cover with boiling water. Leave to stand for 5 minutes, then drain thoroughly.

3　Reheat the wok, add the remaining oil and, when hot, add the pork and stir-fry for 5 minutes or until browned all over. Add the chillies and spring onions and stir-fry for 2 minutes.

4　Add the tomatoes and tofu to the wok with the noodles and coconut mixture and stir-fry for a further 2 minutes, or until heated through, being careful not to break up the tofu. Sprinkle with the chopped coriander and mint, season to taste with salt and pepper and stir. Tip into a warmed serving dish and serve immediately.

Ingredients　　SERVES 4

50 g/2 oz unsalted cashew nuts
1 tbsp ground coriander
1 tbsp ground cumin
2 tsp hot chilli powder
2.5 cm/1 inch piece fresh root
　　ginger, peeled and chopped
1 tbsp oyster sauce
4 tbsp groundnut oil
400 ml/14 fl oz coconut milk
175 g/6 oz rice noodles
450 g/1 lb pork tenderloin,
　　thickly sliced
1 red chilli, deseeded and sliced
1 green chilli, deseeded and sliced
1 bunch spring onions, trimmed and
　　thickly sliced
3 tomatoes, roughly chopped
75 g/3 oz tofu, drained and diced
2 tbsp freshly chopped coriander
2 tbsp freshly chopped mint
salt and freshly ground black pepper

Poultry & Game

Tired of just meat and potatoes? Bored of beef? Try something new with such delectable poultry dishes as Chicken and White Wine Risotto or Persian Chicken Pilaf. Guaranteed, mouths will water for Creamy Caribbean Chicken & Coconut Soup, but if chicken's not your game then Turkey Escalopes Marsala with Wilted Watercress is a must try.

Wonton Noodle Soup

1 Place the mushrooms in a bowl, cover with warm water and leave to soak for 1 hour. Drain, remove and discard the stalks and finely chop the mushrooms. Return to the bowl with the prawns, pork, water chestnuts, 2 of the spring onions and the egg white. Season to taste with salt and pepper. Mix well.

2 Mix the cornflour with 1 tablespoon cold water to make a paste. Place a wonton wrapper on a board and, using a pastry brush, brush the edges with the paste. Drop a little less than 1 teaspoon of
the pork mixture in the centre then fold in half to make a triangle, pressing the edges together. Bring the 2 outer corners together, fixing together with a little more paste. Continue until all the pork mixture is used up; you should have 16–20 wontons.

3 Pour the stock into a large, wide saucepan, add the ginger slices and bring to the boil. Add the wontons and simmer for about 5 minutes. Add the noodles and cook for 1 minute. Stir in the pak choi and cook for a further 2 minutes, or until the noodles and pak choi are tender and the wontons have floated to the surface and are cooked through.

4 Ladle the soup into warmed bowls, discarding the ginger. Sprinkle with the remaining sliced spring onion and serve immediately.

Ingredients SERVES 4

4 shiitake mushrooms, wiped
100 g/4 oz raw prawns, peeled and
   finely chopped
100 g/4 oz lean pork mince
4 water chestnuts, finely chopped
4 spring onions, trimmed and
   finely sliced
1 egg white
salt and freshly ground black pepper
1$\frac{1}{2}$ tsp cornflour
1 packet fresh wonton wrappers
1.2 litres/2 pints chicken stock
2 cm/$\frac{3}{4}$ inch piece root ginger,
   peeled and sliced
75 g/3 oz thin egg noodles
100 g/4 oz pak choi, shredded

Food fact

Wonton wrappers are thin, almost see-through sheets of dough made from eggs and flour, about 10 cm/ 4 inches square. Buy them fresh or frozen from larger supermarkets and oriental stores.

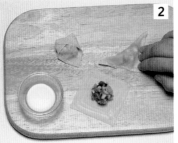

Clear Chicken & Mushroom Soup

1 Skin the chicken legs and remove any fat. Cut each in half to make 2 thigh and 2 drumstick portions and reserve. Heat the groundnut and sesame oils in a large saucepan. Add the sliced onion and cook gently for 10 minutes, or until soft but not beginning to colour.

2 Add the chopped ginger to the saucepan and cook for about 30 seconds, stirring all the time to prevent it sticking, then pour in the stock. Add the chicken pieces and the lemon grass, cover and simmer gently for 15 minutes. Stir in the rice and cook for a further 15 minutes or until the chicken is cooked.

3 Remove the chicken from the saucepan and leave until cool enough to handle. Finely shred the flesh, then return to the saucepan with the mushrooms, spring onions, soy sauce and sherry. Simmer for 5 minutes, or until the rice and mushrooms are tender. Remove the lemon grass.

4 Season the soup to taste with pepper. Ladle into warmed serving bowls, making sure each has an equal amount of shredded chicken and vegetables, and serve immediately.

Ingredients   SERVES 4

2 large chicken legs, about 450 g/1 lb
    total weight
1 tbsp groundnut oil
1 tsp sesame oil
1 onion, peeled and very thinly sliced
2.5 cm/1 inch piece root ginger,
    peeled and very finely chopped
1.1 litres/2 pints clear chicken stock
1 lemon grass stalk, outer leaves
    discarded and bruised
50 g/2 oz long-grain rice
75 g/3 oz button mushrooms, wiped
    and finely sliced
4 spring onions, trimmed, cut into
    5 cm/2 inch pieces and shredded
1 tbsp dark soy sauce
4 tbsp dry sherry
freshly ground black pepper

Chinese Chicken Soup

1 Remove any skin from the chicken. Place on a chopping board and use two forks to tear the chicken into fine shreds.

2 Heat the oil in a large saucepan and fry the spring onions and chilli for 1 minute. Add the garlic and ginger and cook for another minute. Stir in the chicken stock and gradually bring the mixture to the boil.

3 Break up the noodles a little and add to the boiling stock with the carrot. Stir to mix, then reduce the heat to a simmer and cook for 3–4 minutes.

4 Add the shredded chicken, bean sprouts, soy sauce and fish sauce and stir.

5 Cook for a further 2–3 minutes until piping hot. Ladle the soup into bowls and sprinkle with the coriander leaves. Serve immediately.

Ingredients   SERVES 4

225 g/8 oz cooked chicken
1 tsp oil
6 spring onions, trimmed and
    diagonally sliced
1 red chilli, deseeded and
    finely chopped
1 garlic clove, peeled and crushed
2.5 cm/1 inch piece root ginger,
    peeled and finely grated
1 litre/1$^3/_4$ pints chicken stock
150 g/5 oz medium egg noodles
1 carrot, peeled and cut
    into matchsticks
100 g/4 oz bean sprouts
2 tbsp soy sauce
1 tbsp Thai fish sauce
fresh coriander leaves, to garnish

Tasty tip

If possible, buy corn-fed chicken for this recipe. Since this soup is chicken stock-based, the use of corn-fed chicken will make the soup much more flavoursome.

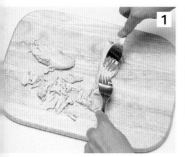

Creamy Caribbean Chicken & Coconut Soup

1 Remove and discard any skin or bones from the cooked chicken, shred using 2 forks and reserve.

2 Heat a large wok, add the oil and, when hot, add the spring onions, garlic and chilli and stir-fry for 2 minutes, or until the onion has softened. Stir in the turmeric and cook for 1 minute.

3 Blend the coconut milk with the chicken stock until smooth, then pour into the wok. Add the pasta or spaghetti with the lemon slices and bring to the boil. Simmer, half-covered, for 10–12 minutes, or until the pasta is tender; stir occasionally.

4 Remove the lemon slices from the wok and add the chicken. Season to taste with salt and pepper and simmer for 2–3 minutes, or until the chicken is heated through thoroughly.

5 Stir in the chopped coriander and ladle into heated bowls. Garnish with sprigs of fresh coriander and serve immediately.

Ingredients   SERVES 4

2 tbsp vegetable oil
6–8 spring onions, trimmed and
    thinly sliced
2 garlic cloves, peeled and
    finely chopped
1 red chilli, deseeded and
    finely chopped
1 tsp ground turmeric
300 ml/$^1/_2$ pint coconut milk
900 ml/1$^1/_2$ pints chicken stock
50 g/2 oz small soup pasta or
    spaghetti, broken into small pieces
$^1/_2$ lemon, sliced
175 g/6 oz cooked chicken meat
salt and freshly ground black pepper
1–2 tbsp freshly chopped coriander
sprigs of fresh coriander, to garnish

Helpful hint

Be careful handling chillies. Either wear rubber gloves or scrub your hands thoroughly, using plenty of soap and water. Avoid touching eyes or any other sensitive areas.

Coconut Chicken Soup

1   Discard the outer leaves from the lemon grass stalks, then place on a chopping board and, using a mallet or rolling pin, pound gently to bruise. Reserve.

2   Heat the vegetable oil in a large saucepan and cook the onions over a medium heat for about 10–15 minutes until soft and beginning to change colour.

3   Lower the heat, stir in the garlic, ginger, lime leaves and turmeric and cook for 1 minute. Add the red pepper, coconut milk, stock, lemon grass and rice. Bring to the boil, cover and simmer gently over a low heat for about 10 minutes.

4   Cut the chicken into bite-sized pieces, then stir into the soup with the sweetcorn kernels and the freshly chopped coriander. Add a few dashes of the Thai fish sauce to taste, then reheat gently, stirring frequently. Serve immediately garnished with a few pickled chillies.

Ingredients   SERVES 4

2 lemon grass stalks
3 tbsp vegetable oil
3 onions, peeled and finely sliced
3 garlic cloves, peeled and crushed
2 tbsp finely grated, fresh root ginger
2–3 kaffir lime leaves
$1\frac{1}{2}$ tsp ground turmeric
1 red pepper, deseeded and diced
400 ml/14 fl oz can coconut milk
1.1 litres/2 pints vegetable or
   chicken stock
250 g/9 oz easy-cook long-grain rice
250 g/9 oz cooked chicken meat
285 g/10 oz can sweetcorn
   kernels. drained
3 tbsp freshly chopped coriander
1-3 tsp or to taste Thai fish sauce
pickled chillies, to garnish

Food fact

If you have difficulty finding kaffir lime leaves, substitute a large strip of lime or lemon rind instead, remembering to remove before serving.

Hot-&-Sour Soup

1
Place the dried shiitake mushrooms in a small bowl and pour over enough almost boiling water to cover. Leave for 20 minutes to soften, then gently lift out and squeeze out the liquid. (Lifting out the mushrooms leaves any sand and grit behind.) Discard the stems, thinly slice the caps and reserve.

2
Heat a large wok, add the oil and, when hot, add the carrot strips and stir-fry for 2–3 minutes, or until beginning to soften. Add the chestnut mushrooms and stir-fry for 2–3 minutes, or until golden, then stir in the garlic and dried chillies.

3
Add the chicken stock to the vegetables and bring to the boil, skimming any foam that rises to the surface. Add the shredded chicken or pork, tofu, if using, spring onions, sugar, vinegar, soy sauce and reserved shiitake mushrooms and simmer for 5 minutes, stirring occasionally. Adjust the seasoning.

4
Blend the cornflour with 1 tablespoon cold water to form a smooth paste and whisk into the soup. Return to the boil and simmer over a medium heat until thickened.

5
Beat the egg with the sesame oil and add to the soup in a slow, steady stream, stirring constantly. Stir in the chopped coriander and serve the soup immediately.

Ingredients   SERVES 4–6

25 g/1 oz dried shiitake mushrooms
2 tbsp groundnut oil
1 carrot, peeled and cut into
    julienne strips
100 g/4 oz chestnut mushrooms,
    wiped and thinly sliced
2 garlic cloves, peeled and finely chopped
$^1/_2$ tsp crushed dried chillies
1.1 litres/2 pints chicken stock
75 g/3 oz cooked boneless chicken
    or pork, shredded
100 g/4 oz firm tofu, thinly
    sliced (optional)
2–3 spring onions, trimmed and finely
    sliced diagonally
1–2 tsp sugar
3 tbsp cider vinegar
2 tbsp soy sauce
freshly ground black pepper
1 tbsp cornflour
1 large egg
2 tsp sesame oil
2 tbsp freshly chopped coriander

Chicken Marengo Casserole

1 Preheat the oven to 180°C/350°F/Gas Mark 4. Lightly rinse the chicken and pat dry on absorbent kitchen paper.

2 Heat the oil and butter in an ovenproof casserole (or frying pan, if preferred), add the chicken portions and cook until browned all over. Remove with a slotted spoon and reserve.

3 Add the onion and garlic and cook gently for 5 minutes, stirring occasionally. Sprinkle in the flour and cook for 2 minutes before stirring in the stock and bringing to the boil.

4 If a frying pan has been used, transfer everything to a casserole, and return the chicken to the casserole with the peeled tomatoes. Season to taste with salt and pepper and add the bay leaf. Cover with a lid and cook in the oven for 30 minutes. Remove the casserole from the oven and add the potatoes and sweetcorn. Return to the oven and cook for 30 minutes. Add the spinach and stir gently through the casserole. Return to the oven and cook for a further 10 minutes, or until the spinach has wilted. Serve.

Ingredients   SERVES 4

4 chicken portions, skinned
1 tbsp olive oil
15 g/½ oz unsalted butter
1 onion, peeled and cut into wedges
2–3 garlic cloves, peeled and sliced
2 tbsp plain flour
900 ml/1½ pints chicken stock
300 g/10 oz tomatoes, peeled
salt and freshly ground black pepper
1 fresh bay leaf
350 g/12 oz new potatoes, scrubbed
    and cut in half
75 g/3 oz sweetcorn kernels
350 g/12 oz fresh spinach

Helpful hint

This can also be made using half chicken stock and half wine.
Use a dry white such as Chardonnay or Pinot Grigio.

Chicken Chasseur

1 Preheat the oven to 180°C/350°F/Gas Mark 4. Skin the chicken, if preferred, and rinse lightly. Pat dry on absorbent kitchen paper. Heat the oil and butter in an ovenproof casserole (or frying pan, if preferred), add the chicken portions and cook, in batches, until browned all over. Remove with a slotted spoon and reserve.

2 Add the onions, garlic and celery to the casserole and cook for 5 minutes, or until golden. Cut the mushrooms in half if large, then add to the casserole and cook for 2 minutes.

3 Sprinkle in the flour and cook for 2 minutes, then gradually stir in the wine. Blend the tomato purée with a little of the stock in a small bowl, then stir into the casserole together with the remaining stock. Bring to the boil, stirring constantly.

4 If a frying pan has been used, transfer everything to a casserole, Return the chicken to the casserole, season to taste and add a few tarragon sprigs.

5 Stir in the sweet potato, cover with a lid and cook in the oven for 30 minutes. Remove the casserole from the oven and add the broad beans. Return to the oven and cook for a further 15–20 minutes, or until the chicken and vegetables are cooked. Serve sprinkled with chopped tarragon.

Ingredients   SERVES 4

1 whole chicken, about 1.5 kg/3 lb in weight, jointed into 4 or 8 portions
1 tbsp olive oil
15 g/½ oz unsalted butter
12 baby onions, peeled
2–4 garlic cloves, peeled and sliced
2 celery sticks, trimmed and sliced
175 g/6 oz closed cup mushrooms, wiped
2 tbsp plain flour
300 ml/½ pint dry white wine
2 tbsp tomato purée
450 ml/¾ pint chicken stock
salt and freshly ground black pepper
few sprigs of fresh tarragon
350 g/12 oz sweet potatoes, peeled and cut into chunks
300 g/10 oz shelled fresh or frozen broad beans
1 tbsp freshly chopped tarragon, to garnish

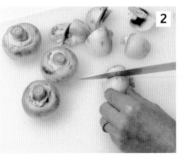

Chicken Creole

1 Lightly rinse the chicken and pat dry on absorbent kitchen paper. Cut the chicken into thin strips. Heat 1 tablespoon of the oil in a deep frying pan, add the chicken and sauté for 5–7 minutes, or until sealed. Remove with a slotted spoon and reserve.

2 Add the remaining oil, if necessary, then add the leeks, onion, garlic and rice and cook, stirring constantly, for 5 minutes. Add all the spices and herbs and cook for a further 5 minutes.

3 Return the chicken to the pan and add the chopped tomatoes. Add half the stock and bring to the boil. Reduce the heat to a simmer and cook for 25 minutes, adding more stock if necessary. Stir in the okra and cook for a further 10 minutes, then serve.

Ingredients   SERVES 4

450 g/1 lb skinless, chicken
    breast fillets
1–2 tbsp olive oil
225 g/8 oz leeks, trimmed and sliced
1 onion, peeled and chopped
3–4 garlic cloves, peeled
    and chopped
200 g/7 oz long-grain rice
$\frac{1}{2}$ tsp cayenne pepper
$1\frac{1}{2}$ tsp paprika pepper
$1\frac{1}{2}$ tsp dried oregano
$1\frac{1}{2}$ tsp dried thyme
225 g/8 oz ripe tomatoes, chopped
900 ml/1$\frac{1}{2}$ pints chicken stock
175 g/6 oz okra, trimmed and sliced

Helpful hint

Okra is used frequently in Creole dishes and will help to thicken the dish slightly. If you cannot find okra, replace with sliced French beans, which although will not thicken, will give an attractive finish to the dish.

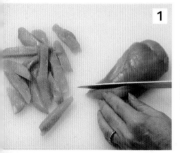

Chicken Gumbo

1 Rinse the chicken portions and pat dry on absorbent kitchen paper. Heat the oil and butter in a large, heavy-based saucepan, add the chicken and fry in batches for 8–10 minutes, or until lightly browned. Remove with a slotted spoon or metal tongs and reserve.

2 Add all the vegetables to the pan and sauté for 8 minutes, or until the vegetables are beginning to soften. Remove with a slotted spoon and reserve.

3 Add the sausages to the pan and cook for 5–8 minutes, or until browned all over, then remove and cut each sausage in half. Return to the pan together with the browned chicken. Add half the browned vegetables and sprinkle in the flour. Cook for 2 minutes then gradually stir in half the stock. Bring to the boil, then reduce the heat, cover and simmer for 40 minutes. Add the remaining vegetables together with the remaining stock and a few dashes of Tabasco and cook for 10 minutes. Stir in the spring onions.

4 Heat the rice according to the packet instructions, then place a serving in a deep bowl. Ladle a portion of the gumbo over the rice and serve.

Ingredients SERVES 4

8 small chicken portions, skinned
1 tbsp olive oil
15 g/½ oz unsalted butter
1 onion, peeled and chopped
2–3 garlic cloves, peeled and chopped
1–2 red chillies, deseeded
   and chopped
2 celery sticks, trimmed and sliced
1 red pepper, deseeded
   and chopped
225 g/8 oz okra, trimmed and sliced
4 spicy sausages
2 tbsp plain flour
1.7 litres/3 pints chicken stock
few dashes of Tabasco sauce
6 spring onions, trimmed
   and chopped
2 x 250 g/9 oz packets precooked
   basmati rice, to serve

Food fact:

Gumbos vary from area to area and there are no rules, so the ingredients can vary according to the region and availability of the ingredients.

Chicken Basquaise

1 Rinse then dry the chicken pieces well with absorbent kitchen paper. Put the flour in a polythene bag, season with salt and pepper and add the chicken pieces. Twist the bag to seal, then shake to coat the chicken pieces thoroughly.

2 Heat $1\frac{1}{2}$ tablespoons of the oil in a large, heavy-based saucepan over a medium-high heat. Add the chicken pieces and cook for about 15 minutes, turning on all sides, until well browned. Using a slotted spoon, transfer to a plate.

3 Add the remaining olive oil to the saucepan, then add the onion and peppers. Reduce the heat to medium and cook, stirring frequently, until starting to colour and soften. Stir in the garlic and chorizo and continue to cook for a further 3 minutes. Add the rice and cook for about 2 minutes, stirring to coat with the oil, until the rice is translucent and golden.

4 Stir in the stock, crushed chillies, thyme, tomato purée and salt and pepper and bring to the boil. Return the chicken to the saucepan, pressing gently into the rice. Cover and cook over a very low heat for about 45 minutes until the chicken and rice are cooked and tender.

5 Gently stir in the ham, black olives and half the parsley. Cover and heat for a further 5 minutes. Sprinkle with the remaining parsley and serve immediately.

Ingredients

SERVES 4–6

1.4 kg/3 lb chicken, cut into 8 pieces
2 tbsp plain flour
salt and freshly ground black pepper
2 tbsp olive oil
1 large onion, peeled and sliced
2 red peppers, deseeded and cut into thick strips
2 garlic cloves, peeled and crushed
150 g/5 oz spicy chorizo sausage, cut into 1 cm/$\frac{1}{2}$ inch pieces
200 g/7 oz long-grain white rice
450 ml/$\frac{3}{4}$ pint chicken stock
1 tsp crushed dried chillies
$\frac{1}{2}$ tsp dried thyme
1 tbsp tomato purée
100 g/4 oz Spanish air-dried ham, diced
12 black olives
2 tbsp freshly chopped parsley

Helpful hint

Look for olives that are already pitted and avoid those that have been marinated in a very spicy marinade, as this could affect the taste of the finished dish.

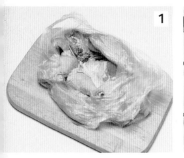

Chicken & Seafood Risotto

1 Heat half the oil in a 45 cm/18 inch paella pan or deep wide frying pan. Add the chicken pieces and fry for 15 minutes, turning constantly, until golden. Remove from the pan and reserve. Add the chorizo and ham to the pan and cook for 6 minutes until crisp, stirring occasionally. Remove and add to the chicken.

2 Add the onion to the pan and cook for 3 minutes, or until beginning to soften. Add the peppers and garlic and cook for 2 minutes; add to the reserved chicken, chorizo and ham.

3 Add the remaining oil to the pan and stir in the rice until well coated. Stir in the bay leaves, thyme and saffron, then pour in the wine and bubble until evaporated, stirring and scraping up any bits on the bottom of the pan. Stir in the stock and bring to the boil, stirring occasionally.

4 Return the chicken, chorizo, ham and vegetables to the pan, burying them gently in the rice. Season to taste with salt and pepper. Reduce the heat and simmer for 10 minutes, stirring occasionally.

5 Add the peas and seafood, pushing them gently into the rice. Cover and cook over a low heat for 5 minutes, or until the rice and prawns are tender and the clams and mussels open (discard any that do not open). Leave to stand for 5 minutes. Sprinkle with the parsley, garnish with lemon wedges and serve.

Ingredients
SERVES 6–8

125 ml/4 fl oz olive oil
1.4 kg/3 lb chicken, cut into 8 pieces
350 g/12 oz spicy chorizo sausage,
    cut into 1 cm/$^1/_2$ inch pieces
100 g/4 oz cured ham, diced
1 onion, peeled and chopped
2 red or yellow peppers, deseeded and
    cut into 2.5 cm/1 inch pieces
4 garlic cloves, peeled and finely chopped
750 g/1 lb 10 oz short-grain Spanish
    rice or risotto rice
2 bay leaves
1 tsp dried thyme
1 tsp saffron strands, lightly crushed
200 ml/7 fl oz dry white wine
1.6 litres/2$^3/_4$ pints chicken stock
salt and freshly ground black pepper
100 g/4 oz fresh shelled peas
450 g/1 lb uncooked prawns
36 clams and/or mussels, well scrubbed
2 tbsp freshly chopped parsley

To garnish:
lemon wedges
fresh parsley sprigs

Chicken & White Wine Risotto

1 Heat the oil and half the butter in a large, heavy-based saucepan over a medium-high heat. Add the shallots and cook for 2 minutes, or until softened, stirring frequently. Add the rice and cook for 2–3 minutes, stirring frequently, until the rice is translucent and well coated.

2 Pour in half the wine; it will bubble and steam rapidly. Cook, stirring constantly, until the liquid is absorbed. Add a ladleful of the hot stock and cook until the liquid is absorbed. Carefully stir in the chicken.

3 Continue adding the stock, about half a ladleful at a time, allowing each addition to be absorbed before adding the next; never allow the rice to cook dry. This process should take about 20 minutes. The risotto should have a creamy consistency and the rice should be tender, but firm to the bite.

4 Stir in the remaining wine and cook for 2–3 minutes. Remove from the heat and stir in the remaining butter with the Parmesan cheese and half the chopped herbs. Season to taste with salt and pepper. Spoon into warmed shallow bowls and sprinkle each with the remaining chopped herbs. Serve immediately.

Ingredients   SERVES 4–6

2 tbsp oil
100 g/4 oz unsalted butter
2 shallots, peeled and finely chopped
300 g/10 oz risotto rice
600 ml/1 pint dry white wine
750 ml/1¼ pints chicken
    stock, heated
350 g/12 oz skinless chicken breast
    fillets, thinly sliced
50 g/2 oz Parmesan cheese, grated
2 tbsp freshly chopped dill or parsley
salt and freshly ground black pepper

Helpful hint

Keep the stock to be added to the risotto at a low simmer in a separate saucepan, so that it is piping hot when added to the rice. This will ensure that the dish is kept at a constant heat during cooking, which is important to achieve the perfect creamy texture.

Pad Thai

1 To make the sauce, whisk all the sauce ingredients in a bowl and reserve. Put the rice noodles in a large bowl and pour over enough hot water to cover. Leave to stand for about 15 minutes until softened. Drain and rinse, then drain again.

2 Heat a wok and, when hot, add the oil and heat for 30 seconds until hot but not smoking. Add the chicken strips and stir-fry constantly until they begin to colour. Using a slotted spoon, transfer to a plate. Reduce the heat to medium-high.

3 Add the shallots, garlic and spring onions and stir-fry for 1 minute. Stir in the rice noodles, then the reserved sauce; mix well.

4 Add the reserved chicken strips, with the crab meat or prawns and radish, and stir well. Cook for about 5 minutes, stirring frequently, until heated through. If the noodles begin to stick, add a little water.

5 Turn into a large, shallow serving dish and sprinkle with the chopped peanuts, if desired. Serve immediately.

Ingredients   SERVES 4

225 g/8 oz flat rice noodles
2 tbsp vegetable oil
225 g/8 oz skinless chicken breast fillets,
     thinly sliced
4 shallots, peeled and thinly sliced
2 garlic cloves, peeled and
     finely chopped
4 spring onions, trimmed and diagonally
     cut into 5 cm/2 inch pieces
350 g/12 oz fresh white crab meat
     or tiny prawns
2 tbsp preserved or fresh radish, chopped
2–3 tbsp roasted peanuts,
     chopped (optional)

For the sauce:

3 tbsp Thai fish sauce
2–3 tbsp rice vinegar or cider vinegar
1 tbsp chilli bean or oyster sauce
1 tbsp toasted sesame oil
1 tbsp light brown sugar
1 red chilli, deseeded and thinly sliced

Persian Chicken Pilaf

1 Heat the oil in a large, heavy-based saucepan over a medium-high heat. Cook the chicken pieces, in batches, until lightly browned.

2 Add the onions to the saucepan, reduce the heat to medium and cook for 3–5 minutes, stirring frequently, until the onions begin to soften. Return all the browned chicken to the saucepan. Add the cumin and rice and stir to coat the rice. Cook for about 2 minutes until the rice is golden and translucent. Stir in the tomato purée and the saffron strands, then season to taste with salt and pepper.

3 Add the pomegranate juice and stock and bring to the boil, stirring once or twice. Add the apricots or prunes and raisins and stir gently. Reduce the heat to low and cook for 30 minutes until the chicken and rice are tender and the liquid is absorbed.

4 Turn into a shallow serving dish and sprinkle with the chopped mint or parsley. Serve immediately, garnished with pomegranate seeds, if using.

Ingredients   SERVES 6

2–3 tbsp vegetable oil
700 g/1½ lb skinless chicken fillets
   (breast and thighs), cut into 2.5
   cm/1 inch pieces
2 onions, peeled and
   coarsely chopped
1 tsp ground cumin
200 g/7 oz long-grain white rice
1 tbsp tomato purée
1 tsp saffron strands
salt and freshly ground black pepper
100 ml/3½ fl oz pomegranate juice
900 ml/1½ pints chicken stock
100 g/4 oz ready-to-eat dried
   apricots or prunes, halved
2 tbsp raisins
2 tbsp freshly chopped mint
   or parsley
pomegranate seeds, to
   garnish (optional)

Creamy Chicken & Rice Pilau

1 Heat the butter in a large, deep frying pan over a medium-high heat. Add the almonds and pistachios and cook for about 2 minutes, stirring constantly, until golden. Using a slotted spoon, transfer to a plate.

2 Add the chicken pieces to the pan and cook for 5 minutes, or until golden, turning once. Remove from the pan and reserve. Add the oil to the pan and cook the onions for 10 minutes, or until golden, stirring frequently. Stir in the garlic, ginger and spices and cook for 2–3 minutes, stirring.

3 Add 2–3 tablespoons of the yogurt and cook, stirring until the moisture evaporates. Continue adding the yogurt in this way until it is used up.

4 Return the chicken and nuts to the pan and stir. Stir in 125 ml/4 fl oz boiling water and season to taste with salt and pepper. Cook, covered, over a low heat for 10 minutes, until the chicken is tender. Stir in the cream, grapes and half the herbs. Gently fold in the rice. Heat through for 5 minutes and sprinkle with the remaining herbs, then serve.

Ingredients
SERVES 4

50 g/2 oz butter
100 g/3$^{1}/_{2}$ oz flaked almonds
75 g/3 oz unsalted shelled pistachio nuts
4 skinless chicken breast fillets,
   each cut into 4 pieces
1 tbsp vegetable oil
2 onions, peeled and thinly sliced
2 garlic cloves, peeled and
   finely chopped
2.5 cm/1 inch piece fresh root
   ginger, finely chopped
6 green cardamom pods,
   lightly crushed
4–6 whole cloves
2 bay leaves
1 tsp ground coriander
$^{1}/_{2}$ tsp cayenne pepper, or to taste
225 ml/8 fl oz natural yogurt
salt and freshly ground black pepper
225 ml/8 fl oz double cream
225 g/8 oz seedless green grapes,
   halved if large
2 tbsp freshly chopped coriander or mint
350 g/12 oz cooked white basmati rice

Turkey Escalopes Marsala with Wilted Watercress

1 Place each turkey escalope between 2 sheets of baking paper and, using a meat mallet or rolling pin, pound to make an escalope about 3 mm/¹/₈ inch thick. Put the flour in a shallow dish, add the thyme, season to taste with salt and pepper and stir to blend. Coat each escalope lightly on both sides with the flour mixture, then reserve.

2 Heat the oil in a large frying pan, then add the watercress and fry, stirring frequently, for about 2 minutes. Season with salt and pepper. Transfer the watercress to a plate and keep warm.

3 Add half the butter to the pan and, when melted, add the mushrooms. Fry for 4 minutes, or until golden and tender. Remove from the pan and reserve. Add the remaining butter to the pan and, working in batches if necessary, cook the flour-coated escalopes for 2–3 minutes on each side, or until golden and cooked thoroughly, adding the remaining oil, if necessary. Remove from the pan and keep warm. Add the Marsala wine to the pan and stir, scraping up any browned bits from the bottom of the pan. Add the stock or water and bring to the boil over a high heat. Season lightly. Return the escalopes and mushrooms to the pan and reheat gently until piping hot. Divide the warm watercress between 4 serving plates. Arrange 1 escalope over each serving of wilted watercress and spoon over the mushrooms and Marsala sauce. Serve immediately.

Ingredients   SERVES 4

4 turkey escalopes, each about
   150 g/5 oz
25 g/1 oz plain flour
¹/₂ tsp dried thyme
salt and freshly ground black pepper
1–2 tbsp olive oil
100 g/4 oz watercress
40 g/1¹/₂ oz butter
225 g/8 oz mushrooms, wiped
   and quartered
50 ml/2 fl oz dry Marsala wine
50 ml/2 fl oz chicken stock or water

Helpful hint

Turkey escalopes are simply thin slices of turkey breast fillets that have been flattened. If they are unavailable, substitute chicken breasts that have been halved horizontally and flattened between pieces of clingfilm.

Herbed Hasselback Potatoes with Roast Chicken

1 Preheat the oven to 200°C/400°F/Gas Mark 6, about 15 minutes before cooking. Place a chopstick on either side of a potato and, with a sharp knife, cut down through the potato until you reach the chopsticks; take care not to cut right through the potato. Repeat these cuts every 5 mm/$\frac{1}{4}$ inch along the length of the potato. Carefully ease 2–4 of the slices apart and slip in a few rosemary sprigs. Repeat with remaining potatoes. Brush with the oil and season well with salt and pepper.

2 Place the seasoned potatoes in a large roasting tin. Add the parsnips, carrots and leeks to the potatoes in the tin and cover with a wire rack or trivet.

3 Beat the butter and lemon rind together and season to taste. Smear the chicken with the lemon butter and place on the rack over the vegetables.

4 Roast in the preheated oven for 1 hour 40 minutes, basting the chicken and vegetables occasionally, until cooked thoroughly. The juices should run clear when the thigh is pierced with a skewer. Place the cooked chicken on a warmed serving platter, arrange the roast vegetables around it and serve immediately.

Ingredients   SERVES 4–6

8 evenly sized potatoes, peeled
3 large sprigs of fresh rosemary
1 tbsp oil
salt and freshly ground black pepper
350 g/12 oz baby parsnips, peeled
350 g/12 oz baby carrots, peeled
350 g/12 oz baby leeks, trimmed
50 g/2 oz softened butter
finely grated rind of 1 lemon,
    preferably unwaxed
1.6 kg/3$\frac{1}{2}$ lb chicken

Food fact

Hasselback potatoes were named after the Stockholm restaurant of the same name. Using chopsticks is a great way of ensuring that you slice just far enough through the potatoes so that they fan out during cooking. The potatoes can be given an attractive golden finish by mixing $\frac{1}{4}$ tsp ground turmeric or paprika with the oil.

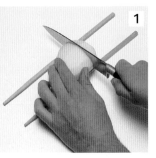

Braised Chicken in Beer

1 Preheat the oven to 190°C/375°F/Gas Mark 5. Cut each chicken joint in half, rinse lightly and pat dry with absorbent kitchen paper. Put in an ovenproof casserole with the prunes and bay leaves.

2 Heat the oil in a large nonstick frying pan. Add the shallots and cook gently for about 5 minutes until beginning to colour.

3 Add the mushrooms to the pan and cook for a further 3–4 minutes until both the mushrooms and onions are softened.

4 Sprinkle the sugar over the shallots and mushrooms, then add the mustard, tomato purée, ale and chicken stock. Season to taste with salt and pepper and bring to the boil, stirring to combine. Carefully pour over the chicken.

5 Cover the casserole and cook in the preheated oven for 1 hour. Blend the cornflour with the lemon juice and 1 tablespoon of cold water and stir into the chicken casserole.

6 Return the casserole to the oven for a further 10 minutes or until the chicken is cooked and the vegetables are tender. Remove the bay leaves and stir in the chopped parsley. Garnish the chicken with the flat-leaf parsley and serve.

Ingredients SERVES 4

4 chicken joints, skinned
100 g/4 oz pitted dried prunes
2 bay leaves
2 tsp olive oil
12 shallots, peeled
100 g/4 oz small button
   mushrooms, wiped
1 tsp soft dark brown sugar
$1/2$ tsp wholegrain mustard
2 tsp tomato purée
150 ml/$1/4$ pint light ale
150 ml/$1/4$ pint chicken stock
salt and freshly ground black pepper
2 tsp cornflour
2 tsp lemon juice
2 tbsp freshly chopped parsley
flat-leaf parsley, to garnish

Helpful hint

To peel the shallots, put in a small bowl and cover with boiling water. Drain the shallots after 2 minutes and rinse under cold water until cool enough to handle. The skins should then peel away easily.

Chicken Baked in a Salt Crust

1 Preheat the oven to 190°C/375°F/Gas Mark 5. Rinse the chicken with cold water and dry well, inside and out, with absorbent kitchen paper. Sprinkle the inside with salt and pepper. Put the onion inside with the rosemary, thyme and bay leaf.

2 Mix the butter, garlic, paprika and lemon rind together. Starting at the neck end, gently ease the skin from the chicken and push the mixture underneath.

3 To make the salt crust, put the flour and salts in a large mixing bowl and stir together. Make a well in the centre. Pour in 600 ml/1 pint cold water and the oil. Mix to a stiff dough, then knead on a lightly floured surface for 2–3 minutes. Roll out the pastry to a circle with a diameter of about 51 cm/20 inches. Place the chicken breast-side down in the middle. Lightly brush the edges with water, then fold over to enclose. Pinch the joints together to seal.

4 Put the chicken join side down in a roasting tin and cook in the preheated oven for 2 hours. Remove from the oven and stand for 20 minutes.

5 Break open the hard crust and remove the chicken. Discard the crust. Remove the skin from the chicken, garnish with the fresh herbs and lemon slices and serve immediately.

Ingredients   SERVES 6

1.8 kg/4 lb oven-ready chicken
salt and freshly ground black pepper
1 onion, peeled
sprig of fresh rosemary
sprig of fresh thyme
1 bay leaf
15 g/$^{1}/_{2}$ oz softened, butter
1 garlic clove, peeled and crushed
pinch of ground paprika
finely grated rind of $^{1}/_{2}$ lemon

Salt crust:

900 g/2 lb plain flour
450 g/1 lb fine cooking salt
450 g/1 lb coarse sea salt
2 tbsp oil

To garnish:

fresh herbs
lemon slices

Helpful hint

It is best to avoid eating the skin from the chicken. It is high in fat and also absorbs a lot of salt from the crust.

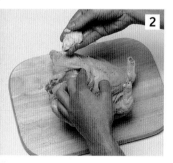

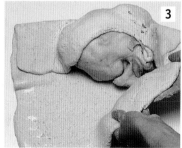

Slow-roast Chicken with Potatoes & Oregano

1 Preheat the oven to 190°C/375°F/Gas Mark 5. Rinse the chicken and dry well, inside and out, with absorbent kitchen paper. Rub the chicken all over with the lemon halves, then squeeze the juice over it and into the cavity. Put the squeezed halves into the cavity with the quartered onion. Rub the softened butter all over the chicken and season to taste with salt and pepper, then put the chicken in a large roasting tin, breast-side down. Toss the potatoes in the oil, season with salt and pepper to taste and add the dried oregano and fresh thyme. Arrange the potatoes with the oil around the chicken and carefully pour 150 ml/¼ pint water into one end of the pan (not over the oil).

2 Roast in the preheated oven for 25 minutes. Turn the chicken breast-side up. Turn the potatoes, sprinkle over half the fresh herbs and baste the chicken and potatoes with the juices. Continue roasting for 1 hour, or until the chicken is thoroughly cooked, basting occasionally. If the liquid evaporates completely, add a little more water. The chicken is done when the juices run clear when the thigh is pierced with a skewer. Transfer the chicken to a carving board and cover with foil or a clean cloth and allow to rest for 5 minutes. Return the potatoes to the oven to keep warm while the chicken is resting. Carve the chicken into serving pieces and arrange on a large heatproof serving dish. Arrange the potatoes around the chicken and drizzle over any remaining juices. Sprinkle with the remaining herbs and serve.

Ingredients SERVES 6

1.4–1.8 kg/3–4 lb oven-ready chicken, preferably free range
1 lemon, halved
1 onion, peeled and quartered
50 g/2 oz softened butter
salt and freshly ground black pepper
1 kg/2 lb 4 oz potatoes, peeled and quartered
3–4 tbsp extra virgin olive oil
1 tbsp dried oregano, crumbled
1 tsp fresh thyme leaves
2 tbsp freshly chopped thyme
fresh sage leaves, to garnish

Helpful hint

When testing if the chicken is cooked, use a clean, long skewer as this will reach the very centre of the thigh.

Turkey Hash with Potato & Beetroot

1 In a large, heavy-based frying pan, heat the oil and half the butter over a medium heat until sizzling. Add the bacon and cook for 4 minutes, or until crisp and golden, stirring occasionally. Using a slotted spoon, transfer to a large bowl. Add the onion to the pan and cook for 5-8 minutes, or until soft and golden, stirring frequently.

2 Meanwhile, add the turkey, potatoes, parsley and flour to the cooked bacon in the bowl. Stir and toss gently, then fold in the diced beetroot.

3 Add half the remaining butter to the frying pan and then the turkey-vegetable mixture. Stir, then spread the mixture to cover the bottom of the frying pan evenly. Cook for 15 minutes, or until the underside is crisp and brown, pressing the hash firmly into a cake with a spatula. Remove from the heat.

4 Invert a large plate over the frying pan and, holding the plate and frying pan together with an oven glove, turn the hash out onto the plate. Heat the remaining butter in the pan, slide the hash back into the pan and cook for 4 minutes, or until crisp and brown on the other side. Invert onto the plate again and serve immediately with a green salad.

Ingredients   SERVES 4

2 tbsp vegetable oil
50 g/2 oz butter
4 slices streaky bacon, rind and cartilage removed, then diced or sliced
1 onion, peeled and finely chopped
450 g/1 lb cooked turkey meat, diced
450 g/1 lb cooked potatoes, sliced
2–3 tbsp freshly chopped parsley
2 tbsp plain flour
250 g/9 oz cooked beetroot, diced
green salad, to serve

Tasty tip

A hash is usually made just with potatoes, but here they are combined with ruby red beetroot, which adds vibrant colour and a sweet earthy flavour to the dish. Make sure that you buy plainly cooked beetroot rather than the type preserved in vinegar.

Sweet & Sour Rice with Chicken

1 Trim the spring onions, then cut lengthways into fine strips. Drop into a bowl of iced water and reserve.

2 Mix together the sesame oil and Chinese five-spice powder and use to rub into the chicken breasts, then cut into small pieces. Heat the wok, then add the vegetable oil and, when hot, cook the garlic and onion for 2–3 minutes, or until transparent and softened.

3 Add the chicken to the wok and stir-fry over a medium-high heat until the chicken is golden and cooked through. Using a slotted spoon, remove from the wok and keep warm.

4 Stir the rice into the wok and add the water, tomato ketchup, tomato purée, honey, carrot, vinegar and soy sauce. Return the chicken to the wok and stir. Bring to the boil, then simmer for 15 minutes or until almost all of the liquid is absorbed. Spoon into a warmed dish. Drain the spring onions and place on top, then serve immediately.

Ingredients   SERVES 4

4 spring onions
2 tsp sesame oil
1 tsp Chinese five-spice powder
450 g/1 lb skinless chicken
   breast fillets
1 tbsp vegetable oil
1 garlic clove, peeled and crushed
1 onion, peeled and sliced into
   thin wedges
225 g/8 oz white basmati rice
600 ml/1 pint water
4 tbsp tomato ketchup
1 tbsp tomato purée
2 tbsp honey
1 tbsp vinegar
1 tbsp dark soy sauce
1 carrot, peeled and cut
   into matchsticks

Food fact

Five-spice powder is a mixture of finely ground star anise, fennel, cinnamon, cloves and Szechuan pepper and adds a unique sweet and spicy aniseed flavour to food.

Chinese-style Fried Rice

1 Heat a wok or large deep frying pan until very hot, add the oil and heat for 30 seconds. Add the onions and stir-fry for 2 minutes. Stir in the garlic and ginger and cook for 1 minute. Add the cooked sliced chicken and ham and stir-fry for a further 2–3 minutes.

2 Add the rice, the water chestnuts and prawns, if using, with 2 tablespoons of water, and stir-fry for 2 minutes until the rice is heated through.

3 Beat the eggs with 1 teaspoon of the sesame oil and season to taste with salt and pepper. Make a well in the centre of the rice, then pour in the egg mixture and stir immediately, gradually drawing the rice mixture into the egg, until the egg is cooked.

4 Add the spring onions, soy and chilli sauces, coriander and a little water, if necessary. Adjust the seasoning and drizzle with the remaining sesame oil. Sprinkle with the peanuts and serve.

Ingredients   SERVES 4–6

2–3 tbsp groundnut or vegetable oil
2 small onions, peeled and cut
     into wedges
2 garlic cloves, peeled and thinly sliced
2.5 cm/1 inch piece fresh root ginger,
     peeled and cut into thin slivers
225 g/8 oz cooked chicken, thinly sliced
100 g/4 oz cooked ham, thinly sliced
350 g/12 oz cooked cold basmati
     white rice
100 g/4 oz canned water chestnuts, sliced
225 g/8 oz cooked peeled
     prawns (optional)
3 large eggs
3 tsp sesame oil
salt and freshly ground black pepper
6 spring onions, trimmed and sliced
     into 1 cm/$^1/_2$ inch pieces
2 tbsp dark soy sauce
1 tbsp sweet chilli sauce
2 tbsp freshly chopped coriander

To garnish:
2 tbsp chopped roasted peanuts
sprig of fresh coriander

Shredded Duck in Lettuce Leaves

1 Cover the dried Chinese mushrooms with almost boiling water, leave for 20 minutes, then drain and slice thinly.

2 Heat a large wok, add the oil and, when hot, stir-fry the duck for 3–4 minutes, or until sealed. Remove with a slotted spoon and reserve. Add the chilli, spring onions, garlic and shiitake mushrooms to the wok and stir-fry for 2–3 minutes, or until softened.

3 Add the bean sprouts, the soy sauce, Chinese rice wine or dry sherry and honey or brown sugar to the wok, and continue to stir-fry for 1 minute, or until blended. Stir in the reserved duck and stir-fry for 2 minutes, or until well mixed together and heated right through. Transfer to a heated serving dish.

4 Pour the hoisin sauce in a small bowl on a tray or plate with a pile of lettuce leaves and the mint leaves. Let each guest spoon a little hoisin sauce onto a lettuce leaf, then top with a large spoonful of the stir-fried duck and vegetables and roll up the leaf to enclose the filling. Serve with the dipping sauce.

Ingredients SERVES 4–6

15 g/¹/₂ oz dried shiitake mushrooms
2 tbsp vegetable oil
400 g/14 oz skinless duck breast fillets, cut crossways into thin strips
1 red chilli, deseeded and cut into thin diagonal slices
4–6 spring onions, trimmed and diagonally sliced
2 garlic cloves, peeled and crushed
75 g/3 oz bean sprouts
3 tbsp soy sauce
1 tbsp Chinese rice wine or dry sherry
1–2 tsp clear honey or brown sugar
4–6 tbsp hoisin sauce

To serve:

large, crisp lettuce leaves, such as iceberg or Cos
handful of fresh mint leaves
plum sauce or sweet chilli sauce to use as a dipping sauce

Thai Chicken Fried Rice

1   Using a sharp knife, trim the chicken, discarding any skin, sinew or fat and cut into small cubes. Reserve.

2   Heat a wok or large frying pan, add the oil and, when hot, add the garlic and cook for 10–20 seconds or until just golden. Add the curry paste and stir-fry for a few seconds. Add the chicken and stir-fry for 3–4 minutes or until tender and the chicken has turned white.

3   Stir the cold cooked rice into the chicken mixture, then add the soy sauce, fish sauce and sugar, stirring well after each addition. Cook, stirring, for 5-8 minutes, or until the chicken is cooked through and the rice is piping hot.

4   Check the seasoning and, if necessary, add a little extra soy sauce. Turn the rice and chicken mixture into a warmed serving dish. Season lightly with black pepper and garnish with shredded spring onion and onion slices. Serve immediately.

Ingredients   SERVES 4

175 g/6 oz chicken breast fillets
2 tbsp vegetable oil
2 garlic cloves, peeled and
    finely chopped
2-3 tsp, or to taste Thai red
    curry paste
450 g/1 lb cold cooked rice
1 tbsp light soy sauce
2 tbsp Thai fish sauce
large pinch of sugar
freshly ground black pepper

To garnish:

2 spring onions, trimmed and
    shredded lengthways
$^1/_2$ small onion, peeled and very
    finely sliced

Helpful hint

Store cooked rice in a refrigerator overnight in a bowl with a tight-fitting lid or clingfilm.

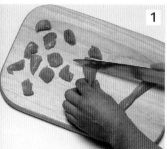

Chicken Chow Mein

1 Place the egg noodles in a large bowl and cover with boiling water. Leave for 3–5 minutes, drain and add 1 tablespoon of the sesame oil and stir lightly. Reserve.

2 Place 2 teaspoons of the light soy sauce, 1 tablespoon of the Chinese rice wine or sherry and 1 teaspoon of the sesame oil with seasoning to taste in a bowl. Add the chicken and stir well. Cover lightly and leave to marinate in the refrigerator for about 15 minutes.

3 Heat the wok over a high heat, add 1 tablespoon of the groundnut oil and, when very hot, add the chicken and its marinade and stir-fry for 2 minutes. Remove the chicken and juices and reserve. Wipe the wok clean with absorbent kitchen paper.

4 Reheat the wok and add the oil. Add the garlic and toss in the oil for 20 seconds. Add the mangetout and the ham and stir-fry for 1 minute. Add the noodles, remaining light soy sauce, Chinese rice wine or sherry, the dark soy sauce and sugar. Season to taste with salt and pepper and stir-fry for 2 minutes.

5 Add the chicken and juices to the wok and stir-fry for 4 minutes, or until the chicken is cooked. Drizzle over the remaining sesame oil. Garnish with spring onions and sesame seeds and serve.

Ingredients   SERVES 4

225 g/8 oz fine egg noodles
5 tsp sesame oil
4 tsp light soy sauce
2 tbsp Chinese rice wine or dry sherry
salt and freshly ground black pepper
225 g/8 oz skinless chicken breast
    fillets, cut into strips
3 tbsp groundnut oil
2 garlic cloves, peeled and
    finely chopped
50 g/2 oz mangetout, finely sliced
50 g/2 oz cooked ham, cut into
    fine strips
2 tsp dark soy sauce
pinch of sugar

To garnish:

shredded spring onions
toasted sesame seeds

Food fact

Sesame oil is a thick, rich, golden brown oil made from toasted sesame seeds. It is used in Chinese cooking mainly as a seasoning.

Noodles with Turkey & Mushrooms

1 Place the noodles in a large bowl and cover with boiling water. Leave for 3-5 minutes, then drain and reserve.

2 Heat the wok, add the oil and, when hot, add the onion and stir-fry for 1 minute. Add the ginger and garlic and stir-fry for a further 3 minutes, then add the turkey strips and stir-fry for 4–5 minutes until sealed and golden.

3 Slice the wild mushrooms into similar-sized pieces and add to the wok with the whole button mushrooms. Stir-fry for 3–4 minutes or until tender. When all the vegetables are tender and the turkey is cooked, add the soy sauce, hoisin sauce, sherry and vegetable stock.

4 Mix the cornflour with 2 tablespoons water and add to the wok, then cook, stirring, until the sauce thickens. Add the drained noodles to the wok, cook, stirring, for 2-3 minutes or until the noodles are hot, then serve immediately.

Ingredients SERVES 4

225 g/8 oz dried fine egg noodles

1 tbsp groundnut oil

1 red onion, peeled and sliced

2 tbsp freshly grated root ginger

3 garlic cloves, peeled and finely chopped

350 g/12 oz skinless turkey breast fillets, cut into strips

150 g/5 oz assorted wild mushrooms, wiped

100 g/4 oz baby button mushrooms, wiped

2 tbsp dark soy sauce

2 tbsp hoisin sauce

2 tbsp dry sherry

4 tbsp vegetable stock

2 tsp cornflour

Helpful hint

When buying wild mushrooms, choose dry-looking specimens without any soft spots. To prepare them, do not wash but brush away any dirt and wipe over gently with a damp cloth. If you cannot find wild mushrooms use chestnut mushrooms.

Chicken & Red Pepper Curried Rice

1 Lightly whisk the egg white with the salt and 2 teaspoons of the cornflour until smooth. Add the chicken and mix together well. Cover and chill in the refrigerator for 20 minutes.

2 Heat a wok and, when hot, add 1 tablespoon of the oil and heat for 30 seconds. Add the chicken mixture to the wok and stir-fry for 2–3 minutes until all the chicken has turned white. Using a slotted spoon, lift the cubes of chicken from the wok, then drain on absorbent kitchen paper.

3 Add the remaining oil to the wok, heat for 30 seconds then add the red pepper and stir-fry for 1 minute over a high heat. Add the curry powder or paste and cook for a further 30 seconds, then add the chicken stock, sugar, Chinese rice wine and soy sauce.

4 Mix the remaining cornflour with 1 teaspoon cold water and add to the wok, stirring. Bring to the boil and simmer gently for 1 minute.

5 Return the chicken to the wok, then simmer for a further 1 minute before adding the rice. Stir over a medium heat for another 2 minutes until heated through. Garnish with the sprigs of coriander and serve.

Ingredients   SERVES 4

1 large egg white
1 tsp salt
1 tbsp cornflour
300 g/10 oz skinless chicken
    breast fillets, cut into chunks
 2 tbsp groundnut oil
1 red pepper, deseeded and
    roughly chopped
1 tbsp curry powder or paste
125 ml/4 fl oz chicken stock
1 tsp sugar
1 tbsp Chinese rice wine or
    dry sherry
1 tbsp light soy sauce
350 g/12 oz cold cooked white rice
sprigs of fresh coriander, to garnish

Helpful hint

Other ingredients can be added to this dish. Try courgettes cut into thin batons, coarsely grated carrot and halved baby corns.

Chicken with Noodles

1 Slice the chicken into fine shreds and mix with 2 teaspoons of the light soy sauce and the Chinese rice wine. Leave to marinate in the refrigerator for 10 minutes.

2 Heat a wok, add 2 teaspoons of the oil and, when hot, stir-fry the chicken shreds for about 2 minutes, then transfer to a plate. Wipe the wok clean with absorbent kitchen paper.

3 Return the wok to the heat and add the remaining oil. Add the garlic, then after 10 seconds add the mangetout and bacon. Stir-fry for a further 1 minute, then add the remaining soy sauce, the sugar and spring onions. Stir-fry for a further 2 minutes, then add the reserved chicken.

4 Add the noodles, stir-fry for a further 3–4 minutes, until the chicken is cooked through and the noodles are hot. Add the sesame oil and mix together. Serve either hot or cold.

Ingredients   SERVES 2–3

100 g/4 oz skinless chicken
    breast fillets
1 tbsp light soy sauce
2 tsp Chinese rice wine or dry sherry
5 tsp groundnut oil
2 garlic cloves, peeled and
    finely chopped
50 g/2 oz mangetout, thinly sliced
25 g/1 oz smoked back bacon, rind
    removed and cut into fine strips
$^1/_2$ tsp sugar
2 spring onions, peeled and
    finely chopped
2 x 150 g/5 oz packs straight-to-wok
    noodles
1 tsp sesame oil

Food fact

Chow mein literally means 'stir-fried noodles'. There are no hard and fast rules about which meat, fish or vegetables can be used. Chow mein also makes a tasty salad if served cold.

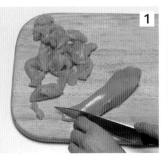

Chicken Wraps

1 Slice the chicken across the grain into 2 cm/³/₄ inch wide strips. Place in a bowl with the lime rind and juice, sugar, oregano, cinnamon and cayenne pepper. Mix well and leave to marinate while making the tortillas.

2 Sift the flour, salt and baking powder into a bowl. Rub in the white fat, then sprinkle over 4 tablespoons warm water and mix to a stiff dough. Knead on a lightly floured surface for 10 minutes until smooth and elastic. Divide the dough into 12 equal pieces and roll each out to a 15 cm/6 inch circle. Cover with clingfilm to prevent drying out.

3 Heat a nonstick wok or large frying pan and cook each tortilla for about 1 minute on each side, or until golden and slightly blistered. Remove the tortillas and keep them warm and pliable in a clean tea towel.

4 Heat 2 tablespoons of the oil in the wok or frying pan and stir-fry the onions for 3 minutes until lightly coloured. Remove with a slotted spoon and reserve. Add the remaining oil to the wok and heat. Drain the chicken from the marinade and add it to the wok. Stir-fry for 5 minutes, then return the onions, add the pepper slices and cook for a further 3–4 minutes, or until the chicken is cooked through and the vegetables are tender. Season to taste with salt and pepper and serve with the tortillas, soured cream and guacamole.

Ingredients   SERVES 4

For the stir-fried chicken:
4 skinless chicken breast fillets
finely grated rind and juice of 1 lime
1 tbsp caster sugar
2 tsp dried oregano
¹/₂ tsp ground cinnamon
¹/₄ tsp cayenne pepper
3 tbsp sunflower oil
2 onions, peeled and sliced
1 green, 1 red and 1 yellow pepper, deseeded and sliced
salt and freshly ground black pepper

For the tortillas:
250 g/9 oz plain flour
pinch of salt
¹/₄ tsp baking powder
50 g/2 oz white vegetable fat

To serve:
soured cream, guacamole

Tasty tip
For a spicy twist add 2 crushed garlic cloves when cooking the onion.

Fish & Seafood

If you love seafood, whether it's Tuna Chowder or Smoked Haddock Rosti, this is the section to stir up something scrumptious. If you're hoping for heat, Thai Hot-&-Sour Prawn Soup or Spicy Cod Rice will not be found lacking. If hot's a not, there's something for everyone, from Pea & Prawn Risotto to restaurant favourites like Bouillabaisse.

Thai Shellfish Soup

1 Peel the prawns. Using a sharp knife, remove the black vein along the back of the prawns. Pat dry with absorbent kitchen paper and reserve. Skin the fish, pat dry and cut into 2.5 cm/ 1 inch chunks. Place in a bowl with the prawns and the squid rings. Sprinkle with the lime juice and reserve.

2 Scrub the mussels, removing their beards and any barnacles. Discard any mussels that are open, damaged or that do not close when tapped. Place in a large bowl and cover with cold water. Change the water frequently before cooking and leave in the refrigerator until required.

3 Place the mussels in a large saucepan and add 150 ml/¹/₄ pint of the coconut milk. Cover, bring to the boil, then simmer for 5 minutes, or until the mussels open, shaking the saucepan occasionally. Lift out the mussels, discarding any unopened ones. Strain the liquid through a muslin-lined sieve and reserve.

4 Rinse and dry the saucepan. Heat the groundnut oil, add the curry paste and cook for 1 minute, stirring all the time. Add the lemon grass, lime leaves and fish sauce and pour in both the strained and the remaining coconut milk. Bring to a very gentle simmer. Add the fish mixture to the saucepan and simmer for 2–3 minutes or until just cooked. Stir in the mussels, with or without their shells, as preferred. Season to taste with salt and pepper, then garnish with coriander leaves. Ladle into warmed bowls and serve.

Ingredients   SERVES 4–6

350 g/12 oz raw prawns
350 g/12 oz firm white fish, such
    as monkfish, cod or haddock
175 g/ 6 oz small squid rings
1 tbsp lime juice
450 g/1 lb live mussels
400 ml/15 fl oz coconut milk
1 tbsp groundnut oil
2 tbsp Thai red curry paste
1 lemon grass stalk, bruised
3 kaffir lime leaves, finely shredded
2 tbsp Thai fish sauce
salt and freshly ground black pepper
fresh coriander leaves, to garnish

Food fact

Sprinkling fish and seafood with lime juice improves its texture, as the acid in the juice firms up the flesh. However do not leave for too long as it will begin to cook the fish.

Thai Hot-&-Sour Prawn Soup

1 Remove the heads from the prawns by twisting away from the body and reserve. Peel the prawns, leaving the tails on and reserve the shells with the heads. Using a sharp knife, remove the black vein from the back of the prawns. Rinse and dry the prawns and reserve. Rinse and dry the heads and shells.

2 Heat a wok, add the oil and, when hot, add the prawn heads and shells, the lemon grass, ginger, garlic, coriander stems and black pepper and stir-fry for 2–3 minutes, or until the prawn heads and shells turn pink and all the ingredients are coloured.

3 Carefully add the water to the wok and return to the boil, skimming off any scum that rises to the surface. Simmer over a medium heat for 10 minutes or until slightly reduced. Strain through a fine sieve and return the clear prawn stock to the cleaned wok.

4 Bring the stock back to the boil and add the reserved prawns, chillies, lime leaves and spring onions and simmer for 3 minutes, or until the prawns turn pink. Season with the fish sauce and lime juice. Spoon into heated soup bowls, dividing the prawns evenly and float a few coriander leaves over the surface.

Ingredients   SERVES 6

700 g/1½ lb large raw prawns
2 tbsp vegetable oil
3–4 lemon grass stalks, outer leaves discarded and coarsely chopped
2.5 cm/1 inch piece fresh root ginger, peeled and finely chopped
2–3 garlic cloves, peeled and crushed
small bunch fresh coriander, leaves stripped and reserved, stems finely chopped
½ tsp freshly ground black pepper
1.8 litres/3¼ pints water
1–2 small red chillies, deseeded and thinly sliced
1–2 small green chillies, deseeded and thinly sliced
6 kaffir lime leaves, thinly shredded
4 spring onions, trimmed and diagonally sliced
1–2 tbsp Thai fish sauce
1–2 tbsp freshly squeezed lime juice

Food fact

Thai fish sauce, made from fermented anchovies, has a sour, salty, fishy flavour.

Sweetcorn & Crab Soup

1 Remove and discard the outer leaves and silky threads from the corn on the cob, if necessary, then rinse and dry. Using a sharp knife and holding the corn cobs at an angle to the cutting board, cut down along the cobs to remove the kernels, then scrape the cobs to remove any excess milky residue. Put the kernels and the milky residue into a large wok.

2 Add the chicken stock to the wok and place over a high heat. Bring to the boil, stirring and pressing some of the kernels against the side of the wok to squeeze out the starch to help thicken the soup. Simmer for 15 minutes, stirring occasionally.

3 Add the spring onions, ginger, Chinese rice wine or dry sherry, soy sauce and brown sugar to the wok and season to taste with salt and pepper. Simmer for a further 5 minutes, stirring occasionally.

4 Blend the cornflour with 1 tablespoon cold water to form a smooth paste and whisk into the soup. Return to the boil, then simmer over medium heat until thickened.

5 Add the crab meat, stirring until blended. Beat the egg white with the sesame oil and stir into the soup in a slow, steady stream, stirring constantly. Stir in the chopped coriander and serve immediately.

Ingredients — SERVES 4

450 g/1 lb fresh corn-on-the-cob
1.3 litres/2^1/$_4$ pints chicken stock
2–3 spring onions, trimmed
    and finely chopped
1 cm/^{1}/$_2$ inch piece fresh root ginger,
    peeled and finely chopped
1 tbsp Chinese rice wine or
    dry sherry
2–3 tsp soy sauce
1 tsp soft light brown sugar
salt and freshly ground black pepper
2 tsp cornflour
225 g/8 oz white crab meat, fresh
    or canned
1 egg white
1 tsp sesame oil
1–2 tbsp freshly chopped coriander

Helpful hint

If fresh crab is unavailable, use thawed frozen or drained canned crab meat. Alternatively, use a mixture of raw shellfish.

Prawn & Chilli Soup

1 To make spring onion curls, finely shred the spring onions lengthways. Place in a bowl of iced cold water and reserve. Remove the heads and shells from the prawns, leaving the tails intact.

2 Split the prawns almost in two to form a butterfly shape and individually remove the black thread that runs down the back of each one.

3 Pour the stock into a large wok or large saucepan and add the lime rind and juice, Thai fish sauce, chilli and soy sauce. Bruise the lemon grass gently by bashing with a rolling pin along its length, then add to the stock and bring to the boil.

4 When the stock mixture is boiling, add the prawns and cook until they are pink. Remove the lemon grass and add the rice vinegar and coriander, then ladle into bowls and garnish with the spring onion curls. Serve immediately.

Ingredients   SERVES 4

2 spring onions, trimmed
225 g/8 oz whole raw tiger prawns
750 ml/1¼ pints fish stock
finely grated rind and juice of 1 lime
1 tbsp Thai fish sauce
1 red chilli, deseeded and chopped
1 tbsp soy sauce
1 lemon grass stalk, outer leaves
   discarded
2 tbsp Chinese rice vinegar
4 tbsp freshly chopped coriander

Tasty tip

For a more substantial dish, cook 50–75 g/2–3 oz Thai fragrant rice for 12–15 minutes, or until just cooked. Drain, then place a little in the soup bowl and ladle the prepared soup on top.

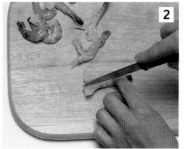

Mediterranean Chowder

1 Heat the oil and butter together in a large saucepan, add the onion, celery and garlic and cook gently for 2–3 minutes until softened. Add the chilli and stir in the flour. Cook, stirring, for a further minute.

2 Add the potatoes to the saucepan with the stock. Bring to the boil, cover and simmer for 10 minutes. Add the fish cubes to the saucepan with the chopped parsley and cook for a further 5–10 minutes, or until the fish and potatoes are just tender.

3 Stir in the peeled prawns and sweetcorn and season to taste with salt and pepper. Pour in the cream and adjust the seasoning, if necessary.

4 Scatter the snipped chives over the top of the chowder. Ladle into 6 large bowls and serve immediately with plenty of warm crusty bread.

Ingredients
SERVES 6

1 tbsp olive oil
15 g/½ oz butter
1 large onion, peeled and
    finely sliced
4 celery sticks, trimmed and
    thinly sliced
2 garlic cloves, peeled and crushed
1 bird's-eye chilli, deseeded and
    finely chopped
1 tbsp plain flour
225 g/8 oz potatoes, peeled
    and diced
900 ml/1½ pints fish or
    vegetable stock
700 g/1½ lb whiting or cod fillet
    cut into 2.5 cm/1 inch cubes
2 tbsp freshly chopped parsley
100 g/4 oz large peeled prawns
198 g/7 oz can sweetcorn, drained
salt and freshly ground black pepper
150 ml/¼ pint single cream
1 tbsp freshly snipped chives
warm crusty bread, to serve

Tuna Chowder

1 Heat the oil in a large, heavy-based saucepan. Add the onion and celery and gently cook for about 5 minutes, stirring from time to time until the onion is softened.

2 Stir in the flour and cook for about 1 minute to thicken. Draw the pan off the heat and gradually pour in the milk, stirring throughout.

3 Add the tuna and its liquid, the drained sweetcorn and the thyme. Mix gently, then bring to the boil. Cover and simmer for 5 minutes.

4 Remove the pan from the heat and season to taste with salt and pepper. Sprinkle the chowder with the cayenne pepper and chopped parsley. Divide into soup bowls and serve immediately.

Ingredients SERVES 4

2 tsp oil
1 onion, peeled and finely chopped
2 celery sticks, trimmed and
   finely sliced
1 tbsp plain flour
750 ml/1¼ pints skimmed milk
200 g/7 oz can tuna in water
320 g/11 oz can sweetcorn in
   water, drained
2 tsp freshly chopped thyme
salt and freshly ground black pepper
pinch cayenne pepper
2 tbsp freshly chopped parsley

Tasty tip

This creamy soup also works well using equivalent amounts of canned crab meat instead of the tuna. For a contrasting taste and to enhance the delicate creaminess of this soup, add a spoonful of low-fat crème fraîche to the top of the soup. Sprinkle with cayenne pepper and then garnish with a few long chives.

Cullen Skink

1 Melt the butter in a large, heavy-based saucepan, add the onion and sauté for 3 minutes, stirring occasionally. Add the bay leaf and stir, then sprinkle in the flour and cook over a low heat for 2 minutes, stirring frequently. Add the potatoes.

2 Take off the heat and gradually stir in the milk and water. Return to the heat and bring to the boil, stirring. Reduce the heat to a simmer and cook for 10 minutes.

3 Meanwhile, discard any pin bones from the fish and cut into small pieces. Add to the pan together with the sweetcorn and peas. Cover and cook gently, stirring occasionally, for 10 minutes, or until the vegetables and fish are cooked.

4 Add pepper and nutmeg to taste, then stir in the cream and heat gently for 1–2 minutes, or until piping hot Sprinkle with the parsley and serve with crusty bread.

Ingredients   SERVES 4

25 g/1 oz unsalted butter
1 onion, peeled and chopped
1 fresh bay leaf
25 g/1 oz plain flour
350 g/12 oz new potatoes, scrubbed
    and cut into small pieces
600 ml/1 pint semi-skimmed milk
300 ml/^{1}/$_2$ pint water
350 g/12 oz undyed smoked
    haddock fillet, skinned
75 g/3 oz sweetcorn kernels
50 g/2 oz garden peas
freshly ground black pepper
^{1}/$_2$ tsp freshly grated nutmeg
2–3 tbsp single cream
2 tbsp freshly chopped parsley
crusty bread, to serve

Tasty tip

Add 100 g/4 oz raw peeled prawns with the cream, if liked. Take care not to overcook or the prawns will lose their flavour and will be tough.

Bouillabaisse

1 Cut the fish into thick pieces, peel the prawns, if necessary, and rinse well. Place the saffron strands in a small bowl, cover with warm water and leave to infuse for at least 10 minutes.

2 Heat the oil in a large, heavy-based saucepan or casserole, add the onions and celery and sauté for 5 minutes, stirring occasionally. Add the tomatoes, bay leaf, garlic and bouquet garni and stir until lightly coated with the oil.

3 Place the firm fish on top of the tomatoes and pour in the saffron-infused water and enough water to just cover. Bring to the boil, reduce the heat, cover with a lid and cook for 8 minutes.

4 Add the soft-flesh fish and continue to simmer for 5 minutes, or until all the fish are cooked. Season to taste with salt and pepper, remove and discard the bouquet garni and serve with French bread.

Ingredients   SERVES 4–6

675 g/1¹/₂ lb assorted fish, such as
    whiting, mackerel, red mullet,
    salmon and king prawns, cleaned
    and skinned
few saffron strands
3 tbsp olive oil
2 onions, peeled and sliced
2 celery sticks, trimmed and sliced
225 g/8 oz ripe tomatoes, peeled
    and chopped
1 fresh bay leaf
2–3 garlic cloves, peeled and crushed
1 bouquet garni
sea salt and freshly ground
    black pepper
French bread, to serve

Tasty tip

Traditionally, eight different fish are used for this dish. Use as many as you wish, but make sure you remove as many bones as possible and use fresh not smoked fish. If liked, use fish stock in place of the water – you will need about 600–750 ml/1–1¹/₄ pints.

Roasted Monkfish with Vegetables

1 Preheat the oven to 190°C/375°F/Gas Mark 5. Cut all the root vegetables, including the onions, into even-sized wedges and place in a large roasting tin. Reserve 2 garlic cloves and add the remainder to the roasting tin. Season to taste with salt and pepper and pour over 1 tablespoon of the oil. Turn the vegetables over until lightly coated in the oil, then roast in the oven for 20 minutes.

2 Meanwhile, cut the monkfish tails into fillets. Using a sharp knife, cut down both sides of the central bone to form 2 fillets from each tail. Discard any skin or membrane, then rinse thoroughly. Make small incisions down the length of the monkfish fillets.

3 Cut the reserved garlic cloves into small slivers and break the rosemary into small sprigs. Insert the garlic and rosemary into the incisions in the fish.

4 Cut the peppers into strips, then add to the roasting tin together with the cherry tomatoes. Place the fish on top and drizzle with the remaining oil. Cook for a further 12–15 minutes, or until the vegetables and fish are thoroughly cooked. Serve sprinkled with chopped parsley.

Ingredients SERVES 4

300 g/10 oz parsnips, peeled
350 g/12 oz sweet potatoes, peeled
300 g/10 oz carrots, peeled
2 onions, peeled
4–6 garlic cloves, peeled
salt and freshly ground black pepper
2 tbsp olive oil
2 small monkfish tails, about 900 g/ 2 lb total weight, or 4 monkfish fillets, about 700 g/1½ lb total weight
2–3 sprigs of fresh rosemary
2 yellow peppers, deseeded
225 g/8 oz cherry tomatoes
2 tbsp freshly chopped parsley

Helpful hint

Other fish can be cooked in this way. If using whole fish, prepare as above, but wrap in nonstick baking paper. If using other fillets, check the cooking time, as most fillets will take slightly less time than the monkfish fillets.

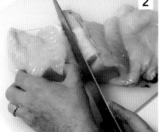

Mediterranean Fish Stew

1 Heat the olive oil in a large saucepan. Add the onion, garlic, fennel and celery and cook over a low heat for 15 minutes, stirring frequently, until the vegetables are soft and just beginning to turn brown.

2 Add the canned tomatoes with their juice, oregano, bay leaf, orange rind and juice with the saffron strands. Bring to the boil, then reduce the heat and simmer for 5 minutes. Add the fish stock, vermouth or wine and season to taste with salt and pepper. Bring to the boil. Reduce the heat and simmer for 20 minutes.

3 Wipe or rinse the haddock and bass fillets and remove as many of the bones as possible. Place on a chopping board and cut into 5 cm/2 inch cubes. Add to the saucepan and cook for 3 minutes. Add the prawns and cook for a further 5 minutes. Adjust the seasoning to taste and serve with crusty bread.

Ingredients SERVES 4–6

3 tbsp olive oil

1 onion, peeled and finely sliced

5 garlic cloves, peeled and finely sliced

1 fennel bulb, trimmed and finely chopped

3 celery sticks, trimmed and finely chopped

400 g/14 oz can chopped tomatoes with Italian herbs

1 tbsp freshly chopped oregano

1 bay leaf

rind and juice of 1 orange

$\frac{1}{2}$ tsp saffron strands

900 ml/1$\frac{1}{2}$ pints fish stock

3 tbsp dry vermouth or white wine

salt and freshly ground black pepper

225 g/8 oz thick haddock fillets, skinned

225 g/8 oz sea bass or bream fillets, skinned

225 g/8 oz raw tiger prawns, peeled

crusty bread, to serve

Chunky Halibut Casserole

 Melt the butter or margarine in a large saucepan, add the onions and pepper and cook for 5 minutes, or until softened.

2 Cut the peeled potatoes into 2.5 cm/1 inch cubes, rinse lightly and shake dry, then add them to the onions and pepper in the saucepan. Add the courgettes and cook, stirring frequently, for a further 2–3 minutes.

3 Sprinkle the flour, paprika and vegetable oil into the saucepan and cook, stirring continuously, for 1 minute. Pour in 150 ml/^{1}/$_4$ pint of the wine, with all the stock and the chopped tomatoes, and bring to the boil.

4 Add the basil to the saucepan, season to taste with salt and pepper and cover. Simmer for 15 minutes, then add the halibut and the remaining wine and simmer very gently for a further 5–7 minutes, or until the fish and vegetables are just tender. Garnish with basil sprigs and serve immediately with freshly heated rice, if using.

Ingredients SERVES 6

50 g/2 oz butter or margarine

2 large onions, peeled and sliced
　into rings

1 red pepper, deseeded and
　roughly chopped

450 g/1 lb potatoes, peeled

450 g/1 lb courgettes, trimmed
　and thickly sliced

2 tbsp plain flour

1 tbsp paprika

2 tsp vegetable oil

300 ml/^{1}/$_2$ pint white wine

150 ml/^{1}/$_4$ pint fish stock

400 g/14 oz can chopped tomatoes

2 tbsp freshly chopped basil

salt and freshly ground black pepper

450 g/1 lb halibut fillet, skinned and
　cut into 2.5 cm/1 inch cubes

sprigs of fresh basil, to garnish

2 x 250 g/9 oz pkts microwaveable
　rice, to serve (optional)

Thai Green Fragrant Mussels

1 Scrub the mussels under cold running water, removing any barnacles and beards. Discard any that have broken or damaged shells or are opened and do not close when tapped gently. Place in a large bowl and cover with cold water. Change the water frequently before cooking and leave in the refrigerator until required.

2 Heat a wok or large frying pan, add the oil and, when hot, add the mussels. Shake gently and cook for 1 minute, then add the garlic, ginger, sliced lemon grass, chillies, green pepper, spring onions, 2 tablespoons of the chopped coriander and the sesame oil.

3 Stir-fry over a medium heat for 3–4 minutes, or until the mussels are cooked and have opened. Discard any mussels that remain unopened.

4 Pour the lime juice with the coconut milk into the wok and bring to the boil. Tip the mussels and the cooking liquor into warmed individual bowls. Sprinkle with the remaining chopped coriander and serve immediately with warm crusty bread.

Ingredients SERVES 4

2 kg/4$\frac{1}{2}$ lb fresh mussels
4 tbsp olive oil
2 garlic cloves, peeled and finely sliced
3 tbsp fresh root ginger, peeled and finely sliced
3 lemon grass stalks, outer leaves discarded and finely sliced
1–3 red or green chillies, deseeded and chopped
1 green pepper, deseeded and diced
5 spring onions, trimmed and finely sliced
3 tbsp freshly chopped coriander
1 tbsp sesame oil
juice of 3 limes
400 ml/14 fl oz can coconut milk
warm crusty bread, to serve

Mussels Arrabbiata

1   Clean the mussels by scrubbing with a small, soft brush, removing the beard and any barnacles from the shells. Discard any mussels that are open or have damaged shells. Place in a large bowl and cover with cold water. Change the water frequently before cooking and leave in the refrigerator until required.

2   Heat the olive oil in a large saucepan and gently fry the onion, garlic and chilli until soft, but not coloured. Add the tomatoes and bring to the boil, then simmer for 15 minutes.

3   Add the white wine to the tomato sauce, bring the sauce to the boil and add the mussels. Cover and carefully shake the pan. Cook the mussels for 5–7 minutes, or until the shells have opened.

4   Add the olives to the pan and cook, uncovered, for about 2 minutes to warm through. Season to taste with salt and pepper and sprinkle in the chopped parsley. Discard any mussels that have not opened and serve immediately with lots of warm crusty bread.

Ingredients   SERVES 4

1.8 kg/4 lb live mussels
3 tbsp olive oil
1 large onion, peeled and sliced
4 garlic cloves, peeled and
    finely chopped
1 red chilli, deseeded and
    finely chopped
3 x 400 g/14 oz cans chopped
    tomatoes
150 ml/¹/₄ pint white wine
175 g/6 oz black olives, pitted
    and halved
salt and freshly ground black pepper
2 tbsp freshly chopped parsley
warm crusty bread, to serve

Food fact

Arrabbiata sauce is a classic Italian tomato-based sauce, usually containing onions, peppers, garlic and fresh herbs. It needs slow simmering to bring out the flavour and is excellent with meat, poultry and pasta as well as seafood.

Seafood Risotto

1 Melt the butter in a large, heavy-based saucepan or frying pan, add the shallots and garlic and cook for 2 minutes until slightly softened. Add the rice and cook for 1–2 minutes, stirring continuously, then pour in the wine, bring to the boil and boil for 1 minute.

2 Pour in half the stock, bring to the boil, cover the saucepan or frying pan and simmer gently for 15 minutes, adding the remaining stock a little at a time and stirring occasionally. Continue to simmer for 5 minutes, or until the rice is cooked and all the liquid is absorbed.

3 Meanwhile, prepare the fish by peeling the prawns and removing the heads and tails. Drain the clams and discard the liquid. Cut the smoked salmon trimmings into thin strips.

4 When the rice has cooked, stir in the prawns, clams, smoked salmon strips and half the chopped parsley, then heat through for 3-4 minutes until everything is piping hot. Turn into a serving dish, sprinkle with the remaining parsley and serve immediately with a green salad and crusty bread.

Ingredients SERVES 4

50 g/2 oz butter
2 shallots, peeled and finely chopped
1 garlic clove, peeled and crushed
350 g/12 oz risotto rice
150 ml/¼ pint white wine
600 ml/1 pint fish or vegetable
  stock, heated
100 g/4 oz large peeled prawns
290 g/10 oz can baby clams
50 g/2 oz smoked salmon trimmings
2 tbsp freshly chopped parsley

To serve:
green salad
crusty bread

Smoked Haddock Rosti

1 Dry the grated potatoes on a clean tea towel. Rinse the grated onion thoroughly in cold water, dry on a clean tea towel and add to the potatoes.

2 Stir the garlic into the potato mixture. Skin the smoked haddock and remove as many of the tiny pin bones as possible. Cut into thin slices and reserve.

3 Heat the oil in a nonstick frying pan. Add half the potato mixture and press well down in the frying pan. Season to taste with salt and pepper.

4 Spread the fish over, then add a sprinkling of lemon rind, parsley and a little black pepper.

5 Top with the remaining potato mixture and press down firmly. Cover with a sheet of foil and cook on the lowest heat for 25–30 minutes.

6 Preheat the grill 2–3 minutes before the end of cooking time. Remove the foil and place the rosti under the grill to brown. Turn out onto a warmed serving dish, and serve immediately with spoonfuls of crème fraîche, lemon wedges and mixed salad leaves.

Ingredients   SERVES 4

450 g/1 lb potatoes, peeled
    and coarsely grated
1 large onion, peeled and
    coarsely grated
2–3 garlic cloves, peeled and crushed
450 g/1 lb smoked haddock
1 tbsp olive oil
salt and freshly ground black pepper
finely grated rind of 1/2 lemon
1 tbsp freshly chopped parsley
2 tbsp half-fat crème fraîche
mixed salad leaves, to garnish
lemon wedges, to serve

Helpful hint

Use smoked haddock fillets. Finnan or arbroath smokies would be too bony for this dish.

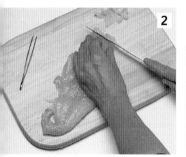

Paella

1. Rinse the mussels under cold running water, scrubbing well to remove any grit and barnacles, then pull off the hairy beards. Tap any open mussels sharply with a knife, and discard if they refuse to close. Place in a large bowl and cover with cold water. Change the water frequently before cooking and leave in the refrigerator until required.

2. Heat the oil in a paella pan or large, heavy-based frying pan and gently cook the chicken thighs for 10–15 minutes until golden. Remove and keep warm.

3. Fry the onion and garlic in the remaining oil in the pan for 2–3 minutes, then add the tomatoes, peppers, peas and paprika and cook for a further 3 minutes. Add the rice to the pan and return the chicken with the turmeric and half the stock. Bring to the boil and simmer, gradually adding more stock as it is absorbed. Cook for 20 minutes, or until most of the stock has been absorbed and the rice is almost tender.

4. Add the mussels to the pan, pressing them gently into the rice. Cook for 5 minutes, then discard any that have not opened, Stir the prawns into the rice. Season to taste with salt and pepper. Heat through for 2–3 minutes until piping hot. Squeeze the juice from 1 of the limes over the paella. Cut the remaining limes and the lemon into wedges and arrange on top of the paella. Sprinkle with the basil, garnish with the prawns and serve.

Ingredients SERVES 6

450 g/1 lb live mussels
4 tbsp olive oil
6 medium chicken thighs
1 onion, peeled and finely chopped
1 garlic clove, peeled and crushed
225 g/8 oz tomatoes, skinned, deseeded and chopped
1 red pepper, deseeded and chopped
1 green pepper, deseeded and chopped
100 g/4 oz frozen peas
1 tsp paprika
450 g/1 lb risotto rice
$^1/_2$ tsp ground turmeric
900 ml/1$^1/_2$ pints chicken stock, warmed
175 g/6 oz large peeled prawns
salt and freshly ground black pepper
2 limes
1 lemon
1 tbsp freshly chopped basil
whole cooked unpeeled prawns, to garnish

Spanish Omelette with Smoked Cod

1. Place the cod in a shallow dish and pour over boiling water. Leave for 5 minutes, then drain and allow to cool, When cool, discard the skin and any pin bones and cut into small pieces.

2. Heat the oil in a large, nonstick, heavy-based frying pan, add the potatoes, onions and garlic and cook gently for 10–15 minutes until golden brown, then add the red pepper. Place the cod on top of the vegetables and cook for 3 minutes.

3. When the vegetables are cooked, drain off any excess oil. Beat the butter and cream into the eggs, then stir in the parsley. Pour the egg mixture over the top of the vegetables and cod and cook gently for 5 minutes, or until the eggs become firm.

4. Sprinkle the grated cheese over the top and place the pan under a preheated hot grill. Cook for 2–3 minutes until the cheese is golden and bubbling. Carefully slide the omelette onto a large plate and serve immediately with plenty of bread and salad.

Ingredients SERVES 3–4

100 g/4 oz smoked cod
3 tbsp sunflower oil
350 g/12 oz potatoes, peeled and
 cut into 1 cm/$^1/_2$ inch cubes
2 onions, peeled and
 cut into wedges
2–4 large garlic cloves, peeled
 and thinly sliced
1 large red pepper, deseeded,
 quartered and thinly sliced
salt and freshly ground black pepper
25 g/1 oz butter, melted
1 tbsp double cream
6 eggs, beaten
2 tbsp freshly chopped
 flat-leaf parsley
50 g/2 oz mature Cheddar
 cheese, grated

To serve:
crusty bread
tossed green salad

Pea & Prawn Risotto

1. Peel the prawns and reserve the heads and shells. Remove the black vein from the back of each prawn, then wash and dry on absorbent kitchen paper.

2. Melt half the butter in a saucepan, add the prawns' heads and shells and fry, stirring occasionally for 3–4 minutes, or until golden. Strain the butter, discard the heads and shells and return the butter to the pan.

3. Add a further 25 g/1 oz of butter to the pan and stir-fry the prawns for 3–4 minutes. Remove from the pan and reserve.

4. Melt the remaining butter in the pan and fry the onion and garlic for 5 minutes until softened, but not coloured. Add the rice and stir the grains in the butter for 1 minute, until they are coated thoroughly. Add the white wine and boil rapidly until the wine is reduced by half.

5. Add the heated stock to the rice, a ladleful at a time. Stir constantly, adding the stock as it is absorbed, until the rice is creamy, but still has a bite in the centre.

6. Stir the cooked prawns into the rice, along with the peas. Add the chopped mint and season to taste with salt and pepper. Cover the pan and leave the prawns to infuse for 5 minutes before serving.

Ingredients SERVES 6

450 g/1 lb whole raw prawns
100 g/4 oz butter
1 red onion, peeled and chopped
4 garlic cloves, peeled and
    finely chopped
225 g/8 oz risotto rice
150 ml/$\frac{1}{4}$ pint dry white wine
1.1 litres/2 pints vegetable or
    fish stock, heated
375 g/13 oz thawed frozen peas
4 tbsp freshly chopped mint
salt and freshly ground black pepper

Tasty tip

Frying the prawn shells and heads before cooking the dish adds a great deal of flavour to the rice. Alternatively, the shells and heads could be added to the stock and simmered for 10 minutes. Strain the stock, pressing the shells and heads well to extract the maximum flavour.

Spicy Cod Rice

1 Mix together the flour, fresh coriander, cumin and ground coriander on a large plate. Coat the cod in the spice mixture then place on a baking sheet, cover and chill in the refrigerator for 30 minutes.

2 Heat a large wok, then add 1 tablespoon of the oil and heat until almost smoking. Stir-fry the cashew nuts for 1 minute, until browned, then remove and reserve.

3 Add a further 1 tablespoon of the oil and heat until almost smoking, add the cod and fry for 2 minutes. Using a fish slice, turn the cod pieces over and cook for a further 2 minutes, until golden. Remove from the wok, place on a warm plate, cover and keep warm.

4 Add the remaining oil to the wok, heat until almost smoking then stir-fry the spring onions and chilli for 1 minute before adding the carrot and peas and stir-frying for a further 2 minutes. Stir in the rice, chilli sauce, soy sauce and cashew nuts and stir-fry for 3 more minutes. Add the cod, heat for 1 minute, then serve immediately.

Ingredients   SERVES 4

1 tbsp plain flour
1 tbsp freshly chopped coriander
1 tsp ground cumin
1 tsp ground coriander
550 g/1¼ lb thick-cut cod fillet, skinned and cut into large chunks
3 tbsp groundnut oil
50 g/2 oz cashew nuts
1 bunch spring onions, trimmed and diagonally sliced
1 red chilli, deseeded and chopped
1 carrot, peeled and cut into matchsticks
100 g/4 oz frozen peas
450 g/1 lb cooked long-grain rice
2 tbsp sweet chilli sauce
2 tbsp soy sauce

Helpful hint

Care is needed when frying nuts as they have a tendency to turn from golden to burnt very quickly. An alternative is to toast them on a baking sheet in the oven at 180°C/350°F/Gas Mark 4 for about 5 minutes until they are golden

Singapore Noodles

1   Put the noodles into a large bowl and pour over boiling
    water to cover. Leave to stand for 3 minutes, or until slightly
    underdone according to the packet instructions. Drain well
    and reserve.

2   Heat a wok until almost smoking. Add the oil and carefully
    swirl around to coat the sides of the wok. Add the shallots,
    garlic and ginger and cook for a few seconds. Add the pepper
    and chilli and stir-fry for 3–4 minutes, or until the pepper
    has softened.

3   Add the prawns, pork, chicken and curry powder to the wok.
    Stir-fry for a further 4–5 minutes until the meat and prawns
    are coloured on all sides, then add the fennel seeds and the
    ground cinnamon and stir to mix.

4   Add the drained noodles to the wok along with the peas and
    cook for a further 2-4 minutes until heated through. Add the
    lemon juice to taste. Sprinkle with the fresh coriander leaves
    and serve immediately.

Ingredients   SERVES 4

225 g/8 oz flat rice noodles
2 tbsp vegetable oil
2 shallots, peeled and sliced
2 garlic cloves, peeled and crushed
2 tbsp freshly grated root ginger
1 red pepper, deseeded and
    finely sliced
1 bird's eye red chilli, deseeded and
    finely chopped
175 g/6 oz peeled raw prawns
100 g/4 oz boneless lean pork, diced
175 g/6 oz boneless chicken, diced
1 tbsp curry powder
1 tsp each crushed fennel seeds and
    ground cinnamon
50 g/2 oz frozen peas, thawed
juice of 1 lemon
3 tbsp fresh coriander leaves

Helpful hint

This is also a great dish for using up
leftover meat, perhaps from the
Sunday roast. If using cooked meat,
reduce the cooking time accordingly,
but make sure that it is piping hot.

Vegetables

Anyone who ever complained of vegetables being flat and flavourless will find themselves singing a different tune after tasting this tongue-tantalizing section. From succulent soups like Carrot & Ginger to choice curries such as Pumpkin & Chickpea, the vegetable will be the most in-demand item on your kitchen's menu.

Potato & Fennel Soup

1 Melt the butter in a large, heavy-based saucepan. Add the onions, with the garlic and half the salt, and cook over a medium heat, stirring occasionally, for 7–10 minutes or until the onions are very soft and beginning to turn brown.

2 Add the potatoes, fennel, caraway seeds and the remaining salt. Cook for about 5 minutes, then pour in the vegetable stock. Bring to the boil, partially cover and simmer for 15–20 minutes or until the potatoes are tender. Stir in the chopped parsley and adjust the seasoning to taste.

3 For a smooth-textured soup, allow to cool slightly then pour into a food processor or blender and blend until smooth. Reheat the soup gently, then ladle into individual soup bowls. For a chunky soup, omit this blending stage and ladle straight from the saucepan into soup bowls.

4 Swirl a spoonful of crème fraîche into each bowl and serve immediately with roughly torn pieces of French stick.

Ingredients   SERVES 4

25 g/1 oz butter
2 large onions, peeled and
   thinly sliced
2–3 garlic cloves, peeled and crushed
$^1/_2$ tsp salt
450 g/1 lb potatoes, peeled and diced
1 fennel bulb, trimmed and
   finely chopped
$^1/_2$ tsp caraway seeds
1 litre/1$^3/_4$ pints vegetable stock
2 tbsp freshly chopped parsley
freshly ground black pepper
4 tbsp crème fraîche
French stick, to serve

Food fact

Fennel has a distinct aniseed flavour, which mellows and sweetens when cooked. Look out for well-rounded bulbs with bright green fronds. Fennel is at its best when fresh, so should be used as soon as possible after buying. It may be stored in the salad drawer of the refrigerator for a few days.

Potato, Leek & Rosemary Soup

1 Melt the butter in a large saucepan, add the leeks and cook gently for 5 minutes, stirring frequently. Remove 1 tablespoon of the cooked leeks and reserve for garnishing.

2 Add the potatoes, vegetable stock, rosemary sprigs and milk. Bring to the boil, then reduce the heat, cover and simmer gently for 20–25 minutes, or until the vegetables are tender.

3 Cool for 5-10 minutes. Discard the rosemary, then pour into a food processor or blender and blend well to form a smooth-textured soup.

4 Return the soup to the cleaned saucepan and stir in the chopped parsley and crème fraîche. Season to taste with salt and pepper. If the soup is too thick, stir in a little more milk or water. Reheat gently without boiling, then ladle into warm soup bowls. Garnish the soup with the reserved leeks and serve immediately with wholemeal rolls.

Ingredients   SERVES 4–6

25 g/1 oz butter
450 g/1 lb leeks, trimmed and
    finely sliced
700 g/1 1/2 lb potatoes, peeled
    and roughly chopped
900 ml/1 1/2 pints vegetable stock
4 sprigs of fresh rosemary
300 ml/1/2 pint milk
2 tbsp freshly chopped parsley
2 tbsp crème fraîche
salt and freshly ground black pepper
wholemeal rolls, to serve

Tasty tip

This rosemary-scented version of Potato and Leek soup is equally delicious served cold, when it would be called Vichyssoise. Allow the soup to cool before covering, then chill in the refrigerator for at least 2 hours. The soup will thicken as it chills, so you may need to thin it to the desired consistency with more milk or stock and season before serving.

Bread & Tomato Soup

1 Make a small cross in the top of each tomato, then place in a bowl and cover with boiling water. Allow to stand for 2 minutes, or until the skins have started to peel away, then drain, remove the skins and seeds and chop into large pieces.

2 Heat the olive oil in a saucepan and gently cook the onion until softened. Add the skinned tomatoes, chopped basil, garlic and chilli powder and season to taste with salt and pepper. Pour in the stock and cover the saucepan. Bring to the boil and simmer gently for 15–20 minutes.

3 Remove the crusts from the bread and break into small pieces. Remove the tomato mixture from the heat and stir in the bread. Cover and leave to stand for 10 minutes, or until the bread has blended with the tomatoes. Season to taste. Serve warm or cold with a swirl of olive oil on the top, garnished with a spoonful of chopped cucumber and some basil leaves.

Ingredients   SERVES 4

900 g/2 lb very ripe tomatoes
3 tbsp olive oil, plus extra for swirling
1 onion, peeled and finely chopped
1 tbsp freshly chopped basil
3 garlic cloves, peeled and crushed
$1/_4$ tsp hot chilli powder
salt and freshly ground black pepper
600 ml/1 pint chicken stock
175 g/6 oz stale white bread

To garnish:

50 g/2 oz cucumber, cut into
   small dice
4 whole basil leaves

Tasty tip

This soup is best made when fresh tomatoes are in season. If you want to make it at other times of the year, replace the fresh tomatoes with 2 x 400 g/14 oz cans peeled plum tomatoes – Italian, if possible. You may need to cook the soup for 5–10 minutes longer.

1

2

3

Rice & Tomato Soup

1 Preheat the oven to 220°C/425°F/Gas Mark 7. Rinse and drain the basmati rice. Place the canned tomatoes with their juice in a large, heavy-based saucepan with the garlic, lime rind, oil and sugar. Season to taste with salt and pepper. Bring to the boil, then reduce the heat, cover and simmer for 10 minutes.

2 Add the vegetable stock or water and the rice and bring to the boil, stirring frequently. Reduce the heat to a simmer and cook, uncovered, for a further 15–20 minutes or until the rice is tender. If the soup is too thick, add a little more water. Reserve and keep warm, if the croutons are not ready.

3 Meanwhile, to make the croutons, mix the pesto and olive oil in a large bowl. Add the bread cubes and toss until they are completely coated with the mixture. Spread on a baking sheet and bake in the preheated oven for 10–15 minutes, until golden and crisp, turning them over halfway through cooking. Serve the soup immediately sprinkled with the warm croutons.

Ingredients SERVES 4

150 g/5 oz easy-cook basmati rice
400 g/14 oz can chopped tomatoes
2 garlic cloves, peeled and crushed
grated rind of 1/2 lime
2 tbsp extra virgin olive oil
1 tsp sugar
salt and freshly ground pepper
900 ml/1 1/2 pints vegetable stock
  or water

For the croutons:
2 tbsp prepared pesto
2 tbsp olive oil
6 thin slices ciabatta bread, cut into
  1 cm/1/2 inch cubes

Helpful hint
If time is short or facilities limited, look out in your local supermarket or grocery store for ready-made croutons. There are now a wide variety of different flavours available.

Lettuce Soup

1 Bring a large saucepan of water to the boil and blanch the lettuce leaves for 3 minutes. Drain and dry thoroughly on absorbent kitchen paper, then shred with a sharp knife.

2 Heat the oil and butter in the cleaned saucepan and add the lettuce, spring onions and parsley and cook together for 3–4 minutes or until very soft.

3 Stir in the flour and cook for 1 minute, then gradually pour in the stock, stirring throughout. Bring to the boil and season to taste with salt and pepper. Reduce the heat, cover and simmer gently for 10–15 minutes or until soft.

4 Allow the soup to cool slightly, then either sieve or purée in a blender. Alternatively, leave the soup chunky. Stir in the cream, add more seasoning, to taste, if liked, then add the cayenne pepper.

5 Arrange the slices of ciabatta bread in a large soup dish or in individual bowls and pour the soup over the bread. Garnish with sprigs of parsley and serve immediately.

Ingredients　　　SERVES 4

2 iceberg lettuces, quartered with hard core removed
1 tbsp olive oil
50 g/2 oz butter
100 g/4 oz spring onions, trimmed and chopped
1 tbsp freshly chopped parsley
1 tbsp plain flour
750 ml/1 1/4 pints chicken stock
salt and freshly ground black pepper
150 ml/1/4 pint single cream
1/4 tsp cayenne pepper, to taste
thick slices stale ciabatta bread
sprig of parsley, to garnish

Helpful hint

Do not prepare the lettuce too far in advance. Iceberg lettuce has a tendency to discolour when sliced, which may in turn discolour the soup.

Cream of Pumpkin Soup

1 Cut the peeled and deseeded pumpkin flesh into 2.5 cm/ 1 inch cubes. Heat the olive oil in a large saucepan and cook the pumpkin for 2–3 minutes, coating it completely with oil.

2 Add the vegetables to the saucepan with the garlic and cook, stirring for 5 minutes or until they have begun to soften. Cover the vegetables with the vegetable stock or water and bring to the boil. Season to taste with salt and pepper and the nutmeg, then cover and simmer for 15–20 minutes or until all of the vegetables are tender.

3 When the vegetables are tender, remove from the heat and cool slightly, then pour into a food processor or blender. Liquidise to form a smooth purée, then pass through a sieve into the cleaned saucepan.

4 Add the cayenne pepper and adjust the seasoning, if necessary. Add all but 2 tablespoons of the cream and a little more water if too thick. Reheat to just below boiling point, then serve immediately swirled with the remaining cream and accompanied by warm herby bread.

Ingredients   SERVES 6–8

900 g/2 lb pumpkin flesh (after
  peeling and discarding the seeds)
4 tbsp olive oil
1 large onion, peeled and
  finely chopped
1 leek, trimmed and
  finely chopped
1 carrot, peeled and diced
2 celery sticks, trimmed and diced
4 garlic cloves, peeled and crushed
1.7 litres/3 pints vegetable stock
  or water
salt and freshly ground black pepper
$1/4$ tsp freshly grated nutmeg
$1/4$ tsp cayenne pepper
150 ml/$1/4$ pint single cream
warm herby bread, to serve

Tasty tip

If you cannot find pumpkin, try replacing it with squash. Butternut, acorn or turban squash would all make suitable substitutes. Avoid spaghetti squash, which is not firm-fleshed when cooked.

1

2

4

Carrot & Ginger Soup

1. Preheat the oven to 180˚C/350˚F/Gas Mark 4. Roughly chop the bread. Dissolve the yeast extract in 2 tablespoons warm water and mix with the bread.

2. Spread the bread cubes over a lightly oiled baking tray and bake for 20 minutes, turning half way through. Remove from the oven and reserve.

3. Heat the oil in a large saucepan. Cook the onion and garlic gently for 3–4 minutes. Stir in the ground ginger and cook for 1 minute to release the flavour.

4. Add the chopped carrots, then stir in the stock and the fresh ginger. Simmer gently for 15 minutes.

5. Remove from the heat and allow to cool a little. Blend until smooth, then season to taste with salt and pepper. Stir in the lemon juice. Garnish with the chives and lemon zest and serve immediately.

Ingredients   SERVES 4

4 slices bread, crusts removed
1 tsp yeast extract
2 tsp olive oil
1 onion, peeled and chopped
1 garlic clove, peeled and crushed
$\frac{1}{2}$ tsp ground ginger
450 g/1 lb carrots, peeled and chopped
1 litre/1$\frac{3}{4}$ pints vegetable stock
2.5 cm/1 inch piece root ginger, peeled and finely grated
salt and freshly ground black pepper
1 tbsp lemon juice

To garnish:
chives
lemon zest

Quick Tip
If time is short or facilities limited, look out in your local supermarket or grocery store for ready made croutons. There are now a wide variety of different flavours available.

Vegetable & Lentil Casserole

1 Preheat the oven to 160 C/325 F/Gas Mark 3. Pour the lentils out onto a plate and look through them for any small stones, then rinse the lentils and reserve.

2 Heat the oil in a large ovenproof casserole (or a deep frying pan, if preferred), add the onion, garlic, carrots and celery and sauté for 5 minutes, stirring occasionally.

3 Add the squash and lentils. Pour in the stock and season to taste with salt and pepper. Add the oregano sprigs and bring to the boil.

4 If a frying pan has been used, transfer everything to a casserole. Cover with a lid and cook in the oven for 25 minutes.

5 Remove the casserole from the oven, add the red pepper and courgettes and stir. Return the casserole to the oven and cook for a further 20 minutes or until all the vegetables are tender. Adjust the seasoning, garnish with sprigs of and serve with soured cream on the side.

Ingredients SERVES 4

225 g/8 oz Puy lentils
1–2 tbsp olive oil
1 onion, peeled and chopped
2–3 garlic cloves, peeled and crushed
300 g/10 oz carrots, peeled and
sliced into chunks
3 celery sticks, trimmed and sliced
350 g/12 oz butternut squash,
peeled, seeds removed and diced
1 litre/1³/₄ pints vegetable stock
salt and freshly ground black pepper
few sprigs of fresh oregano, plus
extra to garnish
1 large red pepper, deseeded
and chopped
2 courgettes, trimmed and sliced
150 ml/¹/₄ pint soured cream,
to serve

Tasty tip

Other vegetables can be added to the casserole, such as sweet potato, aubergine, turnips or parsnips.

Three Bean Tagine

1 Place warm water into a small bowl and sprinkle with saffron strands. Leave to infuse for at least 10 minutes.

2 Heat the oil in a large, heavy-based saucepan, add the aubergine and onion and sauté for 5 minutes before adding the sweet potato, carrots, cinnamon stick and ground cumin. Cook, stirring, until the vegetables are lightly coated in the cumin. Add the saffron with the soaking liquid and season to taste with salt and pepper. Pour in the stock and add the mint sprigs.

3 Rinse the beans, add to the pan and bring to the boil. Reduce the heat, cover with a lid and simmer for 20 minutes. Add the apricots and cook, stirring occasionally, for a further 10 minutes or until the vegetables are tender. Adjust the seasoning to taste, then serve sprinkled with chopped mint.

Ingredients
SERVES 4

few saffron strands
2–3 tbsp olive oil
1 small aubergine, trimmed
and diced
1 onion, peeled and chopped
350 g/12 oz sweet potatoes,
peeled and diced
225 g/8 oz carrots, peeled
and chopped
1 cinnamon stick, bruised
$1\frac{1}{2}$ tsp ground cumin
salt and freshly ground black pepper
600 ml/1 pint vegetable stock
2 sprigs of fresh mint
200 g/7 oz can red kidney
beans, drained
300 g/10 oz can haricot
beans, drained
300 g/10 oz can flageolet
beans, drained
100 g/4 oz ready-to-eat dried
apricots, chopped
1 tbsp freshly chopped mint,
to garnish

Fragrant Vegetable Pot

1 Heat the oil in a large wok or heavy-based saucepan and add the spices, including the chilli. Cook for 2 minutes, stirring constantly.

2 Add the rice and stir until lightly coated in the spices and oil. Pour in half the stock, bring to the boil and cook for 10 minutes.

3 Add the remaining stock, the broccoli, French beans and chopped peppers and cook for a further 10 minutes. Add the sugar snap peas and baby corn and cook for 5–8 minutes, or until the vegetables are tender. Remove and discard the cinnamon stick and star anise and serve sprinkled with chopped coriander, if using.

Ingredients
SERVES 4

1 tbsp groundnut or vegetable oil

1 cinnamon stick, bruised

3 star anise

small piece fresh root ginger, peeled and grated

1 bird's eye red chilli, deseeded and chopped

300 g/10 oz Thai fragrant rice

1.2 litres/2¼ pints vegetable stock

225 g/8 oz broccoli, divided into tiny florets

225 g/8 oz French beans, trimmed and halved

1 red pepper, deseeded and chopped

1 orange pepper, deseeded and chopped

100 g/4 oz sugar snap peas, trimmed

100 g/4 oz baby corn

1 tbsp freshly chopped coriander, to garnish (optional)

Tasty tip

Other fragrant ingredients can be used if you prefer – try lemon grass, bruised green cardamom pods and ground allspice.

Spiced Tomato Pilau

1. Wash the rice in several changes of water until the water remains relatively clear. Drain the rice and cover with fresh water. Leave to soak for 30 minutes. Drain well and reserve.

2. Heat a wok or large frying pan, then melt the butter and add the cardamoms, star anise, cloves, black peppercorns and the cinnamon stick. Cook gently for 30 seconds. Increase the heat and add the onion. Cook for 7–8 minutes, until tender and starting to brown. Add the drained rice and cook for a further 2–3 minutes.

3. Sieve the tomatoes and mix with sufficient warm water to make 450 ml/16 fl oz. Pour this into the wok or frying pan, season to taste with salt and pepper and bring to the boil.

4. Cover, reduce the heat to very low and cook for 10 minutes. Remove from the heat and leave covered for a further 10 minutes. Do not lift the lid during cooking or resting. Finally, uncover and mix well with a fork, then heat for 1 minute. Garnish with the sprigs of fresh coriander and serve immediately.

Ingredients   SERVES 2–3

225 g/8 oz basmati rice

40 g/1$\frac{1}{2}$ oz unsalted butter

4 green cardamom pods

2 star anise

4 whole cloves

10 black peppercorns

5 cm/2 inch piece cinnamon stick

1 large red onion, peeled and
finely sliced

175 g/6 oz canned
chopped tomatoes

salt and freshly ground black pepper

sprigs of fresh coriander, to garnish

Food fact

Star anise is native to south-west China and comes from a small evergreen tree. The spice is actually the fruit of the tree and is harvested just before ripening. It is used extensively in oriental and Indian cuisine, imparting an aromatic anise flavour. It is also used in herbal remedies for coughs and colds, rheumatism and as an aid to digestion.

Bean & Cashew Stir-fry

1. Heat a wok or large frying pan, add the oil and, when hot, add the onion and celery and stir-fry gently for 3–4 minutes or until softened.

2. Add the ginger, garlic and chilli to the wok or frying pan and stir-fry for 30 seconds. Stir in the French beans, mangetout and cashew nuts and continue to stir-fry for 1–2 minutes or until the nuts are golden brown.

3. Dissolve the sugar in the stock, then blend with the sherry, soy sauce and vinegar. Stir into the bean mixture and bring to the boil. Simmer gently, stirring occasionally, for 3–4 minute, or until the beans and mangetout are tender but still crisp and the sauce has thickened slightly. Season to taste with salt and pepper. Transfer to a warmed serving bowl or spoon on to individual plates. Sprinkle with freshly chopped coriander and serve immediately.

Ingredients SERVES 4

2 tbsp vegetable oil

1 onion, peeled and finely chopped

1 celery stick, trimmed and chopped

2.5 cm/1 inch piece fresh root
    ginger, peeled and grated

2 garlic cloves, peeled and crushed

1 red chilli, deseeded and
    finely chopped

175 g/6 oz fine French beans,
    trimmed and halved

175 g/6 oz mangetout,
    sliced diagonally into 3

75 g/3 oz unsalted cashew nuts

1 tsp brown sugar

125 ml/4 fl oz vegetable stock

2 tbsp dry sherry

1 tbsp light soy sauce

1 tsp red wine vinegar

salt and freshly ground black pepper

freshly chopped coriander, to garnish

Courgette & Tarragon Tortilla

1   Peel the potatoes and slice thinly. Dry the slices on a clean tea towel to get them as dry as possible. Heat the 3 tablespoons of oil in a large, heavy-based pan, add the onion and cook for 3 minutes. Add the potatoes with a little salt and pepper, then stir the potatoes and onion lightly to coat in the oil. Reduce the heat to the lowest possible setting, cover and cook gently for 5 minutes. Turn the potatoes and onion over and continue to cook for a further 5 minutes. Give the pan a shake every now and again to ensure that the potatoes do not stick to the base or burn. Add the courgette, then cover and cook for a further 10 minutes.

2   Beat the eggs and tarragon together and season to taste with salt and pepper. Pour the egg mixture over the vegetables and return to the heat. Cook on a low heat for up to 10–15 minutes, or until there is no liquid egg left on the surface of the tortilla.

3   Turn the tortilla over by placing a large plate on top of the pan and, using oven gloves, turning the pan over so the tortilla slips onto the plate. Add the remaining oil to the pan, then slide the tortilla back into the pan.

4   Place the pan under a preheated hot grill. Cook for 2–3 minutes until the surface is golden and bubbling. Carefully slide the tortilla onto a large plate and serve immediately with the tomato wedges and plenty of crusty bread and salad.

Ingredients   SERVES 4

700 g/1¹/₂ lb potatoes
3 tbsp plus 1 tsp olive oil
1 onion, peeled and thinly sliced
salt and freshly ground black pepper
1 courgette, trimmed and
   thinly sliced
6 eggs
2 tbsp freshly chopped tarragon

To serve:
tomato wedges
crusty bread
salad

Food fact

Almost regarded as the national dish of Spain, this substantial omelette is traditionally made from eggs, potatoes and onions. Here, courgettes and tarragon are added for extra flavour and colour. Use even-sized waxy potatoes, which won't break up during cooking – Maris Bard, Charlotte or Pentland Javelin are all good choices of potato.

Beetroot Risotto

1 Heat the oil in a large, heavy-based frying pan. Add the onion, garlic, thyme and lemon rind. Cook gently for 5 minutes, stirring frequently, until the onion is soft and transparent but not coloured. Add the rice and stir until it is well coated in the oil.

2 Add the wine, then bring to the boil and boil rapidly until the wine has almost evaporated. Reduce the heat.

3 Keeping the pan over a low heat, add a ladleful of the hot stock to the rice and cook, stirring constantly, until the stock is absorbed. Continue gradually adding the stock in this way until the rice is tender; this should take about 20 minutes. You may not need all the stock.

4 Stir in the cream, chopped beetroot, parsley and half the grated Parmesan cheese. Season to taste with salt and pepper. Garnish with sprigs of fresh thyme and serve immediately with the remaining grated Parmesan cheese.

Ingredients   SERVES 6

2 tbsp extra virgin olive oil
1 onion, peeled and finely chopped
2 garlic cloves, peeled and
   finely chopped
2 tsp freshly chopped thyme
1 tsp grated lemon rind
350 g/12 oz risotto rice
150 ml/$^1/_4$ pint dry white wine
900 ml/1$^1/_2$ pints vegetable
   stock, heated
2 tbsp double cream
225 g/8 oz cooked beetroot,
   peeled and finely chopped
2 tbsp freshly chopped parsley
75 g/3 oz Parmesan cheese,
   freshly grated
salt and freshly ground black pepper
sprigs of fresh thyme, to garnish

Vegetable Biryani

1 Preheat the oven to 200°C/400°F/Gas Mark 6. Put 1 tablespoon of the vegetable oil in a large bowl with the onions and toss to coat. Lightly brush or spray a nonstick baking sheet with a little more oil. Spread half the onions on the baking sheet and cook at the top of the preheated oven for 25–30 minutes, stirring regularly, until golden and crisp. Remove from the oven and reserve for the garnish.

2 Meanwhile, heat a large ovenproof casserole over a medium heat and add the remaining oil-coated onions. Cook for 5–7 minutes until softened and starting to brown. Add a little water if they start to stick. Add the garlic and ginger and cook for another minute, then add the carrot, parsnip and sweet potato. Cook the vegetables for a further 5 minutes. Add the curry paste and stir for a minute until everything is coated, then stir in the rice and tomatoes. After 2 minutes add the stock and stir well. Bring to the boil, cover and simmer over a very gentle heat for about 10 minutes.

3 Add the cauliflower and peas and cook for 8–10 minutes, or until the rice is tender. Season to taste with salt and pepper. Serve garnished with the crispy onions, cashew nuts, raisins and coriander.

Ingredients   SERVES 4

2 tbsp vegetable oil, plus a little extra
    for brushing
2 large onions, peeled and thinly sliced
2 garlic cloves, peeled and finely
    chopped
2.5 cm/1 inch piece fresh root
    ginger, peeled and finely grated
75g/3 oz carrot, peeled and cut
    into sticks
100 g/4 oz parsnip, peeled and diced
100 g/4 oz sweet potato , peeled
    and diced
1 tbsp medium curry paste
225 g/8 oz basmati rice
4 ripe tomatoes, peeled, deseeded
    and diced
600 ml/1 pint vegetable stock
175 g/6 oz cauliflower florets
50 g/2 oz peas, thawed if frozen
salt and freshly ground black pepper

To garnish:

roasted cashew nuts
raisins
fresh coriander leaves

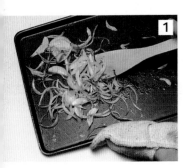

Brown Rice Spiced Pilaf

1. Preheat the oven to 200°C/400°F/Gas Mark 6. Heat the oil in a large ovenproof casserole and add the almonds. Cook for 1–2 minutes until just beginning to brown. (Be very careful as the nuts will burn very easily.)

2. Add the onion and carrot. Cook for 5 minutes until softened and starting to turn brown. Add the mushrooms and cook for a further 5 minutes, stirring often.

3. Add the cinnamon and chilli flakes and cook for about 30 seconds before adding the apricots, currants, orange rind and rice.

4. Gradually stir in the stock and bring to the boil, cover tightly and transfer to the preheated oven. Cook for 45 minutes until the rice and vegetables are tender.

5. Stir the coriander and chives into the pilaf and season to taste with salt and pepper. Garnish with the extra chives and serve immediately.

Ingredients   SERVES 4

1 tbsp vegetable oil
1 tbsp blanched almonds,
    flaked or chopped
1 onion, peeled and chopped
1 carrot, peeled and diced
225 g/8 oz large open mushrooms,
    thickly sliced
$1/4$ tsp ground cinnamon
large pinch crushed chilli flakes
50 g/2 oz dried apricots,
    roughly chopped
25 g/1 oz currants
grated rind of 1 orange
350 g/12 oz brown basmati rice
900 ml/$1^1/_2$ pints vegetable stock
2 tbsp freshly chopped coriander
2 tbsp freshly snipped chives
salt and freshly ground black pepper
snipped chives, to garnish

Food fact
Brown basmati rice is one of the healthiest rices. It slowly releases carbohydrate into the blood thereby maintaining the body's energy levels.

Pumpkin & Chickpea Curry

1 Heat 1 tablespoon of the oil in a medium, heavy-based saucepan and add the onion. Fry gently for 5 minutes until softened.

2 Add the garlic, ginger and spices and fry for a further minute. Add the chopped tomatoes and chillies and cook for a further minute.

3 Add the pumpkin or butternut squash and curry paste and fry gently for 3–4 minutes before stirring in the stock. Bring to the boi and, cover with a lid, then reduce the heat and simmer for 20 minutes or until the pumpkin or butternut squash is tender.

4 Thickly slice the banana and add to the saucepan along with the chickpeas. Simmer for a further 5 minutes.

5 Season to taste with salt and pepper and add the chopped coriander. Serve immediately, garnished with coriander sprigs and some rice or naan bread alongside.

Ingredients   SERVES 4

1 tbsp vegetable oil
1 small onion, peeled and sliced
2 garlic cloves, peeled and
   finely chopped
2.5 cm/1 inch piece root ginger,
   peeled and grated
1 tsp ground coriander
$1/2$ tsp ground cumin
$1/2$ tsp ground turmeric
$1/4$ tsp ground cinnamon
2 tomatoes, chopped
2 red bird's eye chillies,
   deseeded and finely chopped
450 g/1 lb pumpkin or butternut
   squash flesh, cubed
1 tbsp hot curry paste
300 ml/$1/2$ pint vegetable stock
1 large firm banana
400 g/14 oz can chickpeas, drained
   and rinsed
salt and freshly ground black pepper
1 tbsp freshly chopped coriander
coriander sprigs, to garnish
rice or naan bread, to serve

Peperonata

1   Prepare the peppers by halving them lengthways and removing the stems, seeds and membranes. Cut the peppers lengthways into strips about 1 cm/¹/₂ inch wide.

2   Peel the potatoes and cut into slices about 2.5–3 cm/1–1¹/₄ inches. Cut the onion lengthways into 8 wedges.

3   Heat the olive oil in a large saucepan or frying pan over a medium heat. Add the onion and cook for about 5 minutes, or until starting to brown.

4   Add the peppers, potatoes, tomatoes, courgettes, black olives and about 4 torn basil leaves. Season to taste with salt and pepper. Stir the mixture, cover and cook over a very low heat for about 40 minutes, or until the vegetables are tender but still hold their shape.

5   Transfer to a serving bowl, garnish with the remaining basil and serve immediately, with chunks of crusty bread.

Ingredients   SERVES 4-6

2 red peppers
2 yellow peppers
450 g/1 lb waxy potatoes
1 large onion
2 tbsp good-quality virgin olive oil
700 g/1¹/₂ lb tomatoes, peeled,
    deseeded and chopped
2 small courgettes
50 g/2 oz pitted black
    olives, quartered
small handful basil leaves
salt and freshly ground
    black pepper
crusty bread, to serve

Tasty tip

Try serving with Parmesan melba toasts. To make, remove the crusts from 4 slices of thin white bread. Lightly toast and allow to cool before splitting each in half by slicing horizontally. Cut into triangles, place under a grill and toast each side for a few minutes until golden. Sprinkle with finely grated Parmesan and melt under the grill.

Light Ratatouille

1 Deseed the peppers, remove the membrane with a small sharp knife and cut into small dice. Thickly slice the courgettes and cut the aubergine into small dice. Slice the onion into rings.

2 Make a cross on the top of the tomatoes, then place in a large bowl and cover with boiling water. Leave for 1 minute. Drain the tomatoes and, when cool enough to handle, peel. Cut into quarters and remove the seeds.

3 Place all the vegetables in a saucepan with the tomato juice and basil. Season to taste with salt and pepper. Bring to the boil, then cover and simmer for 15 minutes or until the vegetables are tender. Stir occasionally during cooking. Remove the vegetables with a slotted spoon and arrange in a serving dish.

4 Bring the liquid in the pan to the boil and boil for 20 seconds until it is slightly thickened. Adjust the seasoning if necessary. Rub the sauce through a sieve to remove any seeds and pour over the vegetables. Serve the ratatouille hot or cold with crusty bread.

Ingredients   SERVES 4

1 red pepper
2 courgettes, trimmed
1 small aubergine, trimmed
1 onion, peeled
2 ripe tomatoes
50 g/2 oz button mushrooms,
    wiped and halved or quartered
200 ml/7 fl oz tomato juice
1 tbsp freshly chopped basil
salt and freshly ground black pepper
crusty bread, to serve (optional)

Tasty tip

This dish would be perfect, served as an accompaniment to any of the baked fish dishes in this book. It is also delicious in an omelette or as a jacket potato filling.

Creamy Vegetable Korma

1 Heat the ghee or oil in a large saucepan. Add the onion and cook for 5 minutes. Stir in the garlic and ginger and cook for a further 5 minutes or until soft and just beginning to colour.

2 Stir in the cardamom, ground coriander, cumin and turmeric. Continue cooking over a low heat for 1 minute, stirring.

3 Stir in the lemon rind and juice and almonds. Blend in the vegetable stock. Slowly bring to the boil, stirring occasionally.

4 Add the potatoes and mixed vegetables. Bring back to the boil, then reduce the heat, cover and simmer for 35–40 minutes or until the vegetables are just tender. Check after 25 minutes and add a little more stock if needed.

5 Slowly stir in the cream and chopped coriander. Season to taste with salt and pepper. Cook very gently until heated through, but do not boil. Serve immediately with naan bread.

Ingredients   SERVES 4–6

2 tbsp ghee or vegetable oil
1 large onion, peeled and chopped
2 garlic cloves, peeled and crushed
2.5 cm/1 inch piece root ginger,
   peeled and grated
4 cardamom pods, cracked
2 tsp ground coriander
1 tsp ground cumin
1 tsp ground turmeric
finely grated rind and juice
   of $^1/_2$ lemon
50 g/2 oz ground almonds
400 ml/14 fl oz vegetable stock
450 g/1 lb potatoes, peeled
   and diced
450 g/1 lb mixed vegetables, such
   as cauliflower, carrots and turnip,
   cut into chunks
150 ml/$^1/_4$ pint double cream
3 tbsp freshly chopped coriander
salt and freshly ground black pepper
naan bread, to serve

Parsnip Tatin

1 Preheat the oven to 200°C/400°F/Gas Mark 6. Heat the butter in a 20 cm/8 inch frying pan. Add the parsnips, arranging them cut side down with the narrow ends towards the centre.

2 Sprinkle the parsnips with sugar and cook gently for 15 minutes, turning halfway through until golden. Add the apple juice and bring to the boil. Remove the pan from the heat.

3 On a lightly floured surface, roll the pastry out to a size slightly larger than the frying pan. Position the pastry over the parsnips and press down slightly to enclose them.

4 Bake in the preheated oven for 20–25 minutes until the pastry is cooked and golden. Invert a warm serving plate over the pan and, using oven gloves, carefully turn the pan over to flip the tart on to the plate. Serve immediately.

Ingredients   SERVES 4

225 g/8 oz prepared shortcrust pastry

For the filling:
50 g/2 oz butter
8 small parsnips, peeled and halved
1 tbsp brown sugar
75 ml/3 fl oz apple juice

Helpful hint
Take care to choose a frying pan with an ovenproof handle otherwise, use a round 20 cm/8 inch baking tin.

Tasty tip
This dish is delicious served warm with a Greek salad. Feta cheese is one of the main ingredients in Greek salad and because of its salty taste, it tastes particularly good with the creamy flavour of parsnips in this recipe.

Vegetable Cassoulet

1 Preheat the oven to 190°C/375°F/Gas Mark 5. Heat 1 tablespoon of the oil in an ovenproof casserole and add the garlic, onions, carrots, celery and red pepper. Cook gently for 10–12 minutes, until tender and starting to brown. Add a little water if the vegetables start to stick. Add the mushrooms and cook for a further 5 minutes, until softened. Add the herbs and stir briefly.

2 Stir in the red wine and boil rapidly for about 5 minutes, until reduced and syrupy. Stir in the haricot beans, tomato purée and soy sauce. Season to taste with salt and pepper.

3 Mix together the breadcrumbs and parsley with the remaining 1 tablespoon of oil. Scatter this mixture evenly over the top of the cassoulet. Cover loosely with foil and transfer to the preheated oven. Cook for 30 minutes. Carefully remove the foil and cook for a further 15–20 minutes, until the topping is crisp and golden. Serve immediately, garnished with basil sprigs.

Ingredients SERVES 6

2 tbsp olive oil
2 garlic cloves, peeled and chopped
225 g/8 oz baby onions, peeled and halved
150 g/5 oz carrots, peeled and diced
2 celery sticks, trimmed and finely chopped
1 red pepper, deseeded and chopped
175 g/6 oz mixed mushrooms, wiped and sliced
1 tbsp each freshly chopped rosemary, thyme and sage
150 ml/¼ pint red wine
400 g/14 oz can haricot beans, drained and rinsed
4 tbsp tomato purée
1 tbsp dark soy sauce
salt and freshly ground black pepper
50 g/2 oz fresh breadcrumbs
1 tbsp freshly chopped parsley
basil sprigs, to garnish

Thai Noodles & Vegetables with Tofu

1 Drain the tofu well and cut into cubes. Put into a shallow dish with the soy sauce and lime rind. Stir well to coat and leave to marinate for 30 minutes.

2 Meanwhile, put the lemon grass and chilli on a chopping board and bruise with the side of a large knife, ensuring the blade is pointing away from you. Put the vegetable stock in a large saucepan and add the lemon grass, chilli, ginger, garlic and coriander. Bring to the boil, cover and simmer gently for 20 minutes.

3 Strain the stock and return to the rinsed saucepan. Return to the boil and add the noodles, tofu and its marinade and the mushrooms. Simmer gently for 4 minutes.

4 Add the carrots, mangetout, pak choi and coriander and simmer for a further 3–4 minutes, until the vegetables are just tender. Season to taste with salt and pepper. Garnish with coriander sprigs. Serve immediately.

Ingredients   SERVES 4

225 g/8 oz firm tofu
2 tbsp soy sauce
rind of 1 lime, grated
2 lemon grass stalks
1 red chilli
1 litre/1¾ pints vegetable stock
2 slices fresh root ginger, peeled
2 garlic cloves, peeled
2 sprigs of fresh coriander
175 g/6 oz dried thread egg noodles
100 g/4 oz shiitake or button
    mushrooms, sliced if large
2 carrots, peeled and cut
    into matchsticks
100 g/4 oz mangetout
100 g/4 oz pak choi or other
    Chinese leaf
1 tbsp freshly chopped coriander
salt and freshly ground black pepper
coriander sprigs, to garnish

Pad Thai with Mushrooms

1. Place the noodles in a large bowl, cover with boiling water and leave for 3-4 minutes or according to the packet instructions. Drain well and reserve.

2. Heat a wok or large frying pan. Add the oil and garlic and fry until just golden. Add the egg and stir quickly to break it up. Cook for a few seconds before adding the noodles and mushrooms. Scrape down the sides of the pan to ensure they mix with the egg and garlic.

3. Add the lemon juice, fish sauce, sugar, cayenne pepper, spring onions and half of the bean sprouts, stirring quickly all the time. Cook over a high heat for a further 2–3 minutes, until everything is heated through.

4. Turn on to a serving plate. Top with the remaining bean sprouts. Garnish with the chopped peanuts and coriander and serve immediately.

Ingredients SERVES 4

100 g/4 oz flat rice noodles or
  rice vermicelli
1 tbsp vegetable oil
2 garlic cloves, peeled and
  finely chopped
1 egg, lightly beaten
225 g/8 oz mixed mushrooms,
  including shiitake, oyster, field,
  brown and wild mushrooms
2 tbsp lemon juice
1$^{1}/_{2}$ tbsp Thai fish sauce
$^{1}/_{2}$ tsp sugar
$^{1}/_{2}$ tsp cayenne pepper
2 spring onions, trimmed and cut
  into 2.5 cm/1 inch pieces
50 g/2 oz fresh bean sprouts

To garnish:

chopped roasted peanuts
freshly chopped coriander

Rice Nuggets in Herby Tomato Sauce

1   Pour the stock into a large saucepan and add the bay leaf.
    Bring to the boil, then add the rice and stir. Cover and simmer
    for 15 minutes, then uncover, reduce the heat to low and
    cook for a further 5 minutes, until the rice is tender and all
    the stock is absorbed, stirring frequently towards the end of
    the cooking time. Remove from the heat and leave to cool.

2   Stir the cheese, egg yolk, flour and parsley into the rice.
    Season to taste, then shape into 20 walnut-sized balls.
    Cover and refrigerate.

3   To make the sauce, heat the oil in the cleaned saucepan and
    cook the onion for 5 minutes. Add the garlic and yellow
    pepper and cook for a further 3 minutes or until the pepper
    is soft. Stir the chopped tomatoes into the saucepan and
    simmer gently for 3 minutes. Stir in the chopped basil and
    season to taste.

4   Add the rice nuggets to the sauce and simmer for a further
    10 minutes, or until the rice nuggets are cooked through and
    the sauce has reduced a little. Spoon onto serving plates and
    serve hot, sprinkled with grated Parmesan cheese.

Ingredients   SERVES 4

600 ml/1 pint vegetable stock
1 bay leaf
175 g/6 oz risotto rice
50 g/2 oz Cheddar cheese, grated
1 egg yolk
1 tbsp plain flour
2 tbsp freshly chopped parsley
salt and freshly ground black pepper
grated Parmesan cheese, to serve

For the herby tomato sauce: :

1 tbsp olive oil
1 onion, peeled and thinly sliced
1 garlic clove, peeled and crushed
1 small yellow pepper, deseeded
   and diced
400 g/14 oz can chopped tomatoes
1 tbsp freshly chopped basil

Helpful hint

It is important that the stock is absorbed
completely by the rice nuggets. Stir all
the time for the last minute of cooking
to prevent the rice from sticking.

Red Lentil Kedgeree with Avocado & Tomatoes

1. Put the rice and lentils in a sieve and rinse under cold running water. Tip into a bowl, then pour over enough cold water to cover and leave to soak for 10 minutes.

2. Heat the butter and oil in a saucepan. Add the sliced onion and cook gently, stirring occasionally, for 10 minutes, until softened. Stir in the cumin, cardamon pods and bay leaf and cook for a further minute, stirring all the time.

3. Drain the rice and lentils, rinse again and add to the onions in the saucepan. Stir in the vegetable stock and bring to the boil. Reduce the heat, cover the saucepan and simmer for 14–15 minutes or until the rice and lentils are tender.

4. Meanwhile, place the diced avocado in a bowl and toss with the lemon juice. Stir in the tomatoes and chopped coriander. Season to taste with salt and pepper.

5. Once the rice is cooked, fluff it up with a fork, spoon into a warmed serving dish and spoon the avocado mixture on top. Garnish with lemon or lime slices and serve.

Ingredients   SERVES 4

150 g/5 oz basmati rice
150 g/5 oz red lentils
15 g/^{1}/$_2$ oz butter
1 tbsp sunflower oil
1 onion, peeled and chopped
1 tsp ground cumin
4 cardamom pods, bruised
1 bay leaf
450 ml/^{3}/$_4$ pint vegetable stock
1 ripe avocado, peeled,
   stoned and diced
1 tbsp lemon juice
4 plum tomatoes, peeled and diced
2 tbsp freshly chopped coriander
salt and freshly ground black pepper
lemon or lime slices, to garnish

Tasty tip

Although basmati rice and red lentils do not usually need to be pre-soaked, it improves the results of this recipe: the rice will cook to very light, fluffy separate grains and the lentils will just begin to break down, giving a creamier texture.

Index